Building Academic Literacy

Audrey Fielding
Ruth Schoenbach
Marean Jordan

Building Academic Literacy

Lessons from Reading Apprenticeship Classrooms

WestEd Published in Partnership with WestEd

JOSSEY-BASS
A Wiley Imprint
www.josseybass.com

Published by Jossey-Bass
A Wiley Imprint
989 Market Street, San Francisco, CA 94103-1741   www.josseybass.com

Jossey-Bass books and products are available through most bookstores. To contact Jossey-Bass directly call our Customer Care Department within the U.S. at 800-956-7739, outside the U.S. at 317-572-3986 or fax 317-572-4002.

Jossey-Bass also publishes its books in a variety of electronic formats. Some content that appears in print may not be available in electronic books.

Library of Congress Cataloging-in-Publication Data

Building academic literacy : lessons from reading apprenticeship classrooms / edited by Audrey Fielding, Marean Jordan, and Ruth Schoenbach.— 1st ed.
     p. cm. — (Jossey-Bass education series)
Includes bibliographical references and index.
   ISBN 0-7879-6556-1 (alk. paper)
  1. Reading (Secondary)—United States—Curricula—Case studies.   2. Developmental reading—United States—Case studies.   3. Literacy—Social aspects—United States.   I. Fielding, Audrey, 1942-   II. Jordan, Marean. III. Schoenbach, Ruth.   IV. Series.
   LB1632.B77 2003
   428.4'071'2—dc21   2002156220

Printed in the United States of America
FIRST EDITION
PB Printing   10 9 8 7 6 5 4 3 2 1

Contents

Preface ix

Acknowledgments xv

1. Supporting Adolescent Readers: An Introduction
   to the Academic Literacy Course and the
   Reading Apprenticeship Framework 1
   Ruth Schoenbach

2. "A Really Good Conversation": Engaging
   Students in Working with Texts 17
   Daniel Moulthrop

3. Awakening the Reader Within 47
   Lisa Messina, Elizabeth Baker

4. The Voice Inside Your Head Asks, "Are You
   Comprehending?" 91
   Carolyn Orta

5. Creating a Reading Apprenticeship Classroom 101
   Amy Smith

6. Designing an Effective Academic
   Literacy Course 111
   Ruth Schoenbach

Appendix A: Academic Literacy Four-Unit
  Curriculum Matrix   125
Appendix B: Academic Literacy Course Time Line:
  Embedding Routines Across the Year   131
Appendix C: Academic Literacy in English:
  Course Description   133
Appendix D: Academic Literacy, Unit Three:
  Reading History   137
Appendix E: Student Reading Survey   143
Appendix F: Academic Literacy Student
  Competencies   149
Appendix G: Degrees of Reading Power: Test of
  Reading Comprehension   151
Appendix H: Degrees of Reading Power: Readability
  Index for Anthology Selections   153
Notes   161
Bibliography   165
About the Editors   171
About the Sponsor   173
Index   175

Preface

The phone calls started coming in soon after our book *Reading for Understanding: A Guide to Reading in Middle and High School Classrooms* was published in November 1999. That book describes Academic Literacy, a year-long course for all ninth graders in a San Francisco public high school that was designed collaboratively by teachers and researchers in the Strategic Literacy Initiative; its goal is to strengthen students' reading across the academic disciplines. "I've got seven teachers who have all read your book, and we've scheduled the blocks of time for Academic Literacy, but where can we get the student materials?" a panicked high school principal asked a week before school started. Other calls for help came directly from teachers: "I've been trying to find the reading excerpts you list in the appendix of *Reading for Understanding*, but I don't have time to track them all down. Help!"

Building Academic Literacy: An Anthology for Reading Apprenticeship, is a response to those calls for help. The book you hold in your hands is a companion volume to the anthology. The anthology contains readings that support the broad themes in the first unit of the four-unit Academic Literacy course described in *Reading for Understanding*: Unit 1: Reading Self and Society; Unit 2: Reading Media; Unit 3: Reading History; and Unit 4: Reading Science and Technology. (Appendix A in this book provides an overview of the curriculum of these four units.)

Unit 1: Reading Self and Society, the foundational unit of the Academic Literacy course, is designed to engage students in exploring their own and others' personal and social reasons for reading, considering the varied and interrelated processes of reading, and investigating the ways that different types of texts require specialized knowledge and different ways of reading. *Building Academic Literacy: An Anthology for Reading Apprenticeship* is organized into four interrelated themes that make up the content of Unit 1:

Literacy and Identity: Readings focusing on this theme describe the different ways people see themselves as readers and how reading helps shape identity.

Literacy and Power: Readings focusing on this theme show how reading and writing open doors in our lives.

How We Read: Readings on this theme describe the different ways our minds work as we read.

Breaking Codes: Readings on this theme reflect our need to navigate unfamiliar types of texts.

In addition to the calls for help in finding reading materials described in *Reading for Understanding*, we have had similar requests from teachers across the country asking for help in getting started with the kind of Academic Literacy course described in *Reading for Understanding*. "I'm excited to start teaching my first Academic Literacy course," e-mails a veteran teacher, who says the ideas in *Reading for Understanding* confirm her teaching beliefs and practices of many years, "but I'd like to know more about how others have started the course—what kinds of routines are most important to establish first and things like that." Another teacher e-mails with a request for "any ideas about how to help new teachers feel less anxious about teaching a course focused on reading."

This book is a teachers' companion for *An Anthology for Reading Apprenticeship*. It offers detailed pictures of curriculum in courses at two high schools based on the pilot Academic Literacy course at Thurgood Marshall Academic High School described in *Reading for Understanding*. Both of these classroom narratives focus on how teachers begin the Academic Literacy course, working with themes covered by selections in *An Anthology for Reading Apprenticeship*. In addition, this book presents two shorter pieces from middle school teachers who have worked with the texts in *An Anthology for Reading Apprenticeship* in their English and social studies classes.

We hope that many educators implementing an Academic Literacy course will find inspiration and ideas in the portraits of classrooms in this book, adding to the descriptions of the pilot Academic Literacy course described in *Reading for Understanding*. We also hope that many English and Social Studies teachers, and even some pioneering Science and Math teachers, will find ideas in this book they can translate into their own classroom contexts.

This book builds on the conceptual foundation described in *Reading for Understanding*. For readers who are not familiar with this earlier book, Chapter One summarizes the goals and design of the pilot Academic Literacy course and discusses the Reading Apprenticeship framework that guides this work.

In Chapter Two, a ninth-grade English teacher describes the early weeks of an English course his department has developed based on the Academic Literacy course described in *Reading for Understanding*. The author describes the way he introduces students to sharing their conversation about why and how they read. A unit overview is included.

In Chapter Three, two high school teachers discuss the insights they have gained over the past several years as their Academic Literacy course has evolved to place increasing emphasis on helping students "awaken the reader within" and internalize reading strategies. They provide a detailed description of the opening unit in their Academic Literacy course, describing the key goals, activities, and routines they have established to increase students' independence as readers. A unit overview is included.

In Chapter Four a veteran reading teacher shares her approach to teaching her sixth-grade social studies and English core students to focus on comprehension. She describes her work with one of the selections in *An Anthology for Reading Apprenticeship*: "The Voice Inside Your Head," a poem by Thomas Lux.

In Chapter Five, a new middle school teacher discusses the way she has worked with five selections from *An Anthology for Reading Apprenticeship*. She also describes how she uses Reading Apprenticeship approaches to help students improve comprehension of their social studies textbook.

Chapter Six presents an overview of design guidelines for creating an effective Academic Literacy course.

The appendixes provide a variety of planning and resource documents from the Academic Literacy course described in *Reading for Understanding*:

Appendix A: Academic Literacy Four-Unit Curriculum Matrix, which presents an overview of focus areas, key activities, texts, and student competencies across a year of an Academic Literacy course with the four curriculum units referenced in Chapters One and Six of this book

Appendix B: Academic Literacy Course Time Line: Embedding Routines Across the Year, provides a one-page overview of the ways to introduce the Academic Literacy course routines across the four curriculum units

Appendix C: Academic Literacy in English: Course Description, provides the larger curriculum context for the parts of Daniel Moulthrop's course described in Chapter Two

Appendix D: Academic Literacy Unit 3: Reading History, describes an Academic Literacy curriculum unit that involves students in active exploration of multiple thematically linked texts and can be used to generate ideas for other units based in other disciplines or focused on other themes

Appendix E: Student Reading Survey, described in *Reading for Understanding* and referenced in several chapters of this book

Appendix F: Academic Literacy Student Competencies, a one-page chart that links the Reading Apprenticeship dimensions with goals and examples of what students will know and be able to do through participation in the Academic Literacy course

Appendix G: Degrees of Reading Power Test of Reading Comprehension, describes the reasons the SLI research team chose this particular reading comprehension test and describes what the test measures, how it is constructed, and what the readability index measures

Appendix H: Degrees of Reading Power Readability Index for Anthology Selections, with readability ratings for the selections from *Building Academic Literacy: An Anthology for Reading Apprenticeship*

Audrey Fielding
San Francisco, California

Marean Jordan
Berkeley, California

Ruth Schoenbach
San Francisco, California

Acknowledgments

We thank everyone who contributed to the making of this book. As educators, we recognize and appreciate the wisdom of our colleagues. Early in the book's development, a number of teachers participated in field-testing Reading Apprenticeship readings and processes. We thank them for their enthusiastic and helpful responses. As the concept for the book developed, three of our Reading Apprenticeship colleagues were invaluable as thoughtful readers and advisers: Jane Braunger, Cynthia Greenleaf, and Lori Hurwitz. Margot DeVries, administrative assistant for the Strategic Literacy Initiative, was consistently gracious and efficient as the communications expert for teachers, colleagues, and our publisher. Finally, we thank Christie Hakim, associate editor for education at Jossey-Bass, for her patience, support, and advice.

Building Academic Literacy

Supporting Adolescent Readers

An Introduction to the Academic Literacy Course and the Reading Apprenticeship Framework

Ruth Schoenbach

In the current era of high-stakes testing, conversations about the challenge of improving literacy for middle school and high school youth have become increasingly urgent. The Strategic Literacy Initiative (SLI) of WestEd has been working with communities of middle school and high school subject-area teachers since 1995 to develop new ways to address this complex challenge. Many of the teachers, administrators, and policymakers with whom we discuss the need to improve literacy skills are concerned, as we are, with educational equity and access. A disproportionately high number of African American and Latino adolescents are not receiving the kind of support they need to realize their potential as citizens with a wide repertoire of literacy skills. The vast majority of African American and Latino students who are identified as "struggling readers" are able to decode (sound out) words but struggle to comprehend the broad range of texts they will need to understand in today's information-driven world. Instead of being challenged and strategically supported to build on their existing knowledge resources, they are often consigned to remedial reading classes, which do little to engage their intelligence. This perpetuates an academic achievement gap, limiting too many young people's opportunities and diminishing the contributions they will be able to make to our evolving national and global community.[1]

In spite of recently increased efforts to improve reading outcomes for low-performing students, a pressing question remains:
*How can we help students who see themselves as nonreaders, who may
be alienated from school and school reading in general, become willing
and able readers of a variety of academic texts?*

The work described in the following chapters, situated in classrooms of teachers participating in communities convened and supported by the SLI, addresses this question by starting with the idea
that a sense of self-confidence, self-awareness, and an identity as a
reader are necessary preconditions for increasing students' capacity
to read and respond to academic texts.[2]

An Anthology for Reading Apprenticeship, for which this book is a
companion volume, offers students a rich set of reading resources for
reexamining their reading identities in relation to a wide world of
readers from other times and places. Readings in the four interrelated
themes of *An Anthology for Reading Apprenticeship*—Literacy and
Identity, Literacy and Power, How We Read, and Breaking Codes—
give students a chance to become more curious about and aware of
the differences and similarities in reading experiences across a range
of readers, to see reading as a social activity with social implications,
to examine their assumptions about reading, and to expand their
understandings of the varied kinds of reading that different types of
texts require.

Reading, talking, and writing about the reading lives of people
from a wide cultural and historical spectrum and grappling with the
different kinds of language and thought in varied types of texts can be
powerful not only for students who do not see themselves as readers
of academic texts, but also for more academically oriented students.
Explorations into the themes in *An Anthology for Reading Apprenticeship* can provide opportunities for all students to learn to access more
difficult texts, challenge themselves to read more critically, and begin
to become the kinds of readers colleges and universities expect.

Working to build academic literacy means going beyond helping students learn to pick out main ideas from topic or ending sen-

tences or learning to do a passable summary of a selection of expository text on a high school exit exam. The kinds of reading and writing required for the challenges of college, technical school, work, and civic life and for advanced achievement on the National Educational Assessment Program (NAEP) tests, begin with the active engagement of the reader. At the advanced level, as NAEP defines it, readers are constructing new understandings by interacting within and across texts, summarizing, analyzing, and evaluating. They are using literacy for creative and critical thinking and for problem solving.[3]

The more that readers are able to draw on everything they know as they read and write, the more meaning they are able to make of texts they encounter. As students learn to engage with texts and learn new ways to identify and solve comprehension problems they encounter while they read, their independence and range as readers increase exponentially. They begin to become more active readers too. Students who have never before read an entire book finish their first book; students who have felt that their science or social studies textbooks are "too boring" or "too hard" learn to pay attention to "what goes on in your mind while you are reading" and to visualize, summarize, predict, and make connections to what they read. As students engage more fully, the texts seem to change for them: they start to see that "these people in the history book were *real*. . . . These things *really happened!*" or that "the science book just seems more interesting now." Students who have felt overwhelmed by academic reading begin to understand that reading is problem solving; they start to see that they can work at solving comprehension problems in the types of challenging academic texts that function as gatekeepers in relation to further education and opportunity.

Building academic literacy means building the ability to read critically with reference to other texts and world knowledge, to understand a given text in the broader context of its genre and discipline, and to be able to interpret and apply understanding from the reading. Readers must learn to bridge from what they already know to what is new for them. Building the kinds of confident, critical, and creative academic literacy we envision for students—especially for students who have already labeled themselves or been labeled as "nonreaders"—requires that teachers find explicit and structured ways of raising students' awareness of their reading habits and identities. They must support students as they learn to meet new, rigorous, and interesting literacy challenges. In the vision of academic literacy we hold, motivation and engagement are not ends in themselves. Rather, they constitute the crucial foundation for students' further development as readers and learners.

Academic literacy—the ability to comprehend and read and write critically in a range of academic disciplines—can and should be developed in the context of subject-area classrooms. The bulk of our work with teams of middle school and high school teachers in the San Francisco Bay Area and around the country through National Institutes on Reading Apprenticeship is rooted in the goal of building academic literacy within subject-area classes. Teaching reading in history *is* teaching history, involving explicit modeling and guided practice in reading for point of view, bias, key ideas, and connections to other historical concepts and themes previously discussed and to one's own world knowledge from multiple sources. Similarly, teaching reading in science, mathematics, and literature classes can help students learn the ways of thinking that are valued in these disciplines. In helping students to become more active and engaged readers, pioneering social studies, science, math, and English teachers who are working with the Reading Apprenticeship instructional framework are finding that when they set up a strong personal and social foundation for reading in their disciplines, students are more likely to meet or exceed the cognitive and knowledge development goals they have for them.

Lessons from Reading Apprenticeship Classrooms builds on the conceptual foundation described in *Reading for Understanding: A Guide to Improving Reading in Middle and High School Classrooms*. The rest of this chapter provides a summary of the goals and design of the pilot Academic Literacy course and the Reading Apprenticeship framework introduced in that book, which informs the work described in the following chapters.

The Academic Literacy Course

The Academic Literacy course began in the fall of 1996 as a mandatory course for all incoming ninth graders at Thurgood Marshall Academic High School, a school serving the poorest neighborhoods of San Francisco and established by court decree to provide a college preparatory education for the Latino and African American students who had been historically deprived of such educational opportunities. According to school reports, the 1996–1997 ninth grade at Thurgood Marshall was approximately 30 percent African American, 25 percent Latino, 24 percent Chinese American, 7 percent Filipino, and 8 percent other nonwhite students. Only 3 percent of the students were white. Approximately 7 percent of the ninth-grade students were classified as special education students eligible for support services, and 14 percent were identified as English-language learners.

The school had opened in 1994 with many recent high school reforms in place, including block scheduling, family groupings of students with academic core faculty, and project-based, interdisciplinary teaching and learning. Twelve sections of Academic Literacy met for two ninety-minute block periods and one fifty-minute period per week. Christine Cziko, a veteran English teacher, codesigner, and lead teacher of the course, recruited three other teachers to teach this course, among them a first-year English teacher and two history teachers.

Academic Literacy had three goals: to increase students' engagement, fluency, and competency in reading. The course had a metacognitive and meta-affective focus, placing adolescent students in control of their own engagement and reading practices.[4] Students in the course were invited into an inquiry through a set of essential questions that the course was designed to explore: "What is reading?" "What do proficient readers do when they read?" Students were to gain a greater awareness of their reading and to come to understand their own reading practices and habits: "What are my characteristics as a reader?" "What strategies do I use as I read?" The course was also designed to increase student motivation for reading by revealing, within the students' framework of reference, the power of literacy to shape lives. The students explored questions such as, "What roles does reading serve in people's personal and public lives?" leading to a clearer understanding of the role reading will play in their future educational and career goals and goals they can set and work toward to help themselves develop as readers. Finally, the course had a meta-discourse focus, exploring how texts are designed and conventionally structured through such questions as, "What kind of language is characteristic of this kind of text?" "What does this language and structure demand of the reader?" Students encountered and revisited these questions through a series of units and activities designed to engage them in ideas, strategies, and practices to demystify discipline-based reading and apprentice them as academic readers.

Three units were designed to focus on the role and use of reading in one's personal and public world: Reading Self and Society, Reading Media, and Reading History. Two years later, a fourth unit, Reading Science and Technology, was created. Within these units, specific subject areas provided what we hoped would be compelling content, as well as sites for integration of reading strategies and practices. (See Appendix A for an overview of these four units.)

Throughout the four units of Academic Literacy, teachers modeled and guided students in key instructional strategies. These included sustained silent reading (SSR), reciprocal teaching (RT), and explicit, integrated instruction in self-monitoring, cognitive strategies, and text analysis that would facilitate reading a variety of materials.

In the first unit of the course, Academic Literacy teachers engaged students in practicing the component strategies of RT (questioning, summarizing, clarifying, and predicting) as they read a variety of texts and conducted inquiries into reading. Students were also given specific instruction, as well as modeling and thinking-aloud opportunities, as they examined the features of different text genres. They learned and practiced techniques for note taking, paraphrasing, and using graphic organizers and mapping to identify text structure and support processing of information in texts; identifying root words, prefixes, and suffixes; and developing semantic networks. All strategy and text instruction was embedded in units of subject-area study and the reading of a variety of texts. Critically, the overarching goal of putting students in control of their own engagement in and assessment of these strategies for themselves as readers ran through these instructional routines. Through the shared inquiry into reading, students were encouraged to reappraise their own conceptions of literacy, set and accomplish personal goals for reading development, and draw on the social resources of the classroom community in developing new and more powerful reading repertoires.

Impact of Academic Literacy on Student Reading

SLI's research team, led by Cynthia Greenleaf, worked with the pilot Academic Literacy teachers at Marshall to collect a variety of data, including standardized test scores and qualitative data to gauge student thinking and learning. Standardized measures included pre- and posttests of reading proficiency using the Degrees of Reading Power (DRP) test. Qualitative measures included pre- and post-course reading surveys adapted from Nanci Atwell (Appendix E), as well as student written reflections, self-assessments, and course evaluations; focus group interviews; classroom observations; and samples of course work for thirty students selected randomly from the class rosters of the two of the Academic Literacy teachers.

Student Performance on Standardized Reading Comprehension Tests

Academic Literacy students improved their performance significantly on the DRP test, moving from the forty-seventh to nearly the forty-ninth percentile in national ranking in the seven months of instructional time between October and May of their ninth-grade year.[5] The DRP test is both norm and criterion referenced. In comparison with the national norm, the ninth graders in Academic Literacy classes started the year reading on average at a late seventh-grade level, moving to a late ninth-grade level (catching up to the national norm for ninth graders) by May. In terms of familiar texts, by the test makers' estimate, students were able independently to read and comprehend texts similar in difficulty to *Charlotte's Web*, *Old Yeller*, and children's magazines at the start of the year. By May, the test makers estimate they were able to independently read and comprehend texts similar in difficulty to *To Kill a Mockingbird*, *The Adventures of Tom Sawyer*, and teen reading materials. The increase of nearly 4 units on the DRP criterion-referenced scale from fall to spring is significantly greater than the norm, based on samples of large, national populations of same-grade students. These students' increased average reading levels in May, as estimated by the DRP, suggested that they should be able to handle all but the most difficult high school textbooks with instructional support and that with instructional support, these students should be able to tackle difficult literature like *The Prince* and *The Scarlet Letter*.

Student Responses to Reading Surveys

In addition to the standardized test results, the surveys also tell an aggregate story of students' changed reading habits. For example, students nearly doubled the average number of books they reported reading in the previous twelve months (from 5.58 in fall to 10.99 in spring). The surveys and students' writing also provided more individual glimpses of the impact of the Academic Literacy course for students. After reading his pre- and postsurveys, one student wrote in a reflective letter to his teacher, "Before I didn't consider myself a good reader but now I do. I think that my attitude about reading has changed a lot 'cause since we started reading I got used to it. Now I feel more confident as a reader." In a similar testimony to this changed relationship to reading, a ninth-grade girl wrote, "I've learned this month that I've really started reading very good [sic]. I've done it so much that it's become a custom. I took both of my books everywhere I went. I even took them to Great America with me and read in the lines to get on rides."

The development of the Academic Literacy course took place in the context of a larger two-year teacher-researcher collaboration convened by SLI staff. This collaboration had the goal of creating novel and practical solutions to the complex problem of supporting students' reading in subject-area classrooms. Toward that goal, this teacher-research group worked to synthesize the broad field of reading research, to carry out videotaped and text-based case studies on a set of thirty ninth-grade students, and to find ways to apply research findings to the particular literacy learning and developmental needs of these (and similar) adolescents. As we advanced this program of research-in-practice, we were developing Reading Apprenticeship, a theoretically grounded instructional framework to guide teachers working across a range of disciplines and across a range of student populations.

The Reading Apprenticeship Framework

The Reading Apprenticeship framework, described fully in *Reading for Understanding,* is more than an instructional add-on or additional curriculum. It is, rather, an instructional framework that teachers embed in the process of teaching subject-area content. Its goal is to help students become more active, strategic, and independent readers by (1) supporting students' discovery of their own reasons to read and ways of reading, (2) modeling disciplinary ways of reading in different subject areas and genres, and (3) guiding students to explore, strengthen, and assess their own reading.

Reading Apprenticeship is at heart a partnership of expertise, drawing on what teachers know and do as readers in their disciplines and on adolescents' unique and often underestimated strengths as learners. It helps students become better readers in the following ways:

- Engaging students in more reading

- Making the teacher's discipline-based reading processes and knowledge visible to students

- Making the students' reading processes, knowledge, and understandings visible to the teacher and to one another

- Helping students gain insight into their own reading processes as a means of gaining strategic control over these processes

- Helping students acquire a repertoire of problem-solving strategies for deepening comprehension of texts in various academic disciplines

In a Reading Apprenticeship classroom, the curriculum includes how we read and why we read in the ways we do, as well as what we read in subject matter classes. The Reading Apprenticeship framework, set out in Figure 1.1, involves teachers in orchestrating and integrating four interacting dimensions of classroom life that support reading development: the social, personal, cognitive, and knowledge-building dimensions. These dimensions are woven into subject-area teaching through *metacognitive conversations*, that is, investigations into the thinking processes that students and teachers employ as they read.

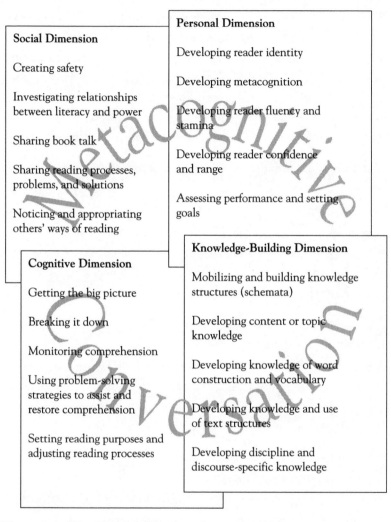

Figure 1.1. Dimensions of Reading Apprenticeship
Source: ©WestEd 2002. All rights reserved.

The Social Dimension: Building a Reading Inquiry Community

The social dimension in the Reading Apprenticeship framework involves developing a sense of safety in the classroom community and making good use of adolescents' interests in peer interactions. As students share confusions and difficulties with texts as well as understandings and ways of solving comprehension problems, they build both content knowledge and a repertoire of reading strategies.

The Personal Dimension: Creating a Sense of Agency

The personal dimension in the Reading Apprenticeship framework involves addressing adolescents' interest in exploring new aspects of their own identities and self-awareness as readers. In this dimension of the framework, students are encouraged to use the strategic skills they use in out-of-school settings to support their ability to be more strategic and purposeful about their reading.

The Cognitive Dimension: Developing a Comprehension Toolkit

The cognitive dimension in the Reading Apprenticeship framework involves developing students' repertoire of specific comprehension and problem-solving strategies, with an emphasis on group discussion of when and why particular cognitive strategies are useful.

The Knowledge-Building Dimension: Accessing and Extending Knowledge

The knowledge-building dimension involves identifying and expanding the knowledge students bring to a text. This includes knowledge about topics and content, text structure, word level knowledge, and discourse patterns and signals—the particular ways ideas are organized and expressed in various different disciplines and genres within each discipline.

Metacognitive Conversation

In Reading Apprenticeship classrooms, the social, personal, cognitive, and knowledge-building dimensions of classroom life are woven into subject-area teaching through ongoing conversation about ways of reading and thinking in that particular discipline. As they engage in conversations about the concepts embedded in reading selections, teachers and students discuss their personal relationships to reading in the discipline, the cognitive strategies they use to solve comprehension problems, the structure and language of particular types of texts, and the kinds of knowledge required to make sense of reading materials in that subject area.

Lessons from Reading Apprenticeship Classrooms: Common Threads

The following four chapters present high school and middle school settings in which teachers are integrating the Reading Apprenticeship framework into their classrooms. Although the ways in which teachers embed the core elements of the framework in their curriculum and work with their students differ, readers may notice common threads that run throughout these classroom narratives.

Metacognitive Conversation

These four chapters all offer images and voices from classrooms illustrating what we describe as metacognitive conversation—conversation that helps students become more aware of the ways they and others process text and of the connections they make to texts. These metacognitive conversations help students learn to manage their attention and interest and to flexibly employ a variety of strategies for refocusing their attention and for solving comprehension problems. In Daniel Moulthrop's ninth-grade English class, for example, we see students in a reciprocal teaching group pausing at the end of each page "to make sure everyone understands what's happening and to share their questions and ideas." In Lisa Messina and Elizabeth Baker's classrooms, we see teachers sharing stories from their own reading histories and listening to students as they talk honestly about what they hate about reading. In Carolyn

Orta's classroom narrative, we hear joking and groans from her sixth-grade students as they chant the oft-repeated "If you're not comprehending, you're not reading!" in preparation for reading a new poem years beyond their grade level. In Amy Smith's classroom, we hear teacher and students sharing their confusions with the texts they read, as the teacher models strategies for solving comprehension problems in a social studies text.

Student Agency

In addition to the common thread of metacognitive conversation across these classrooms, we also see a shared focus on what we describe as students' *agency*—their increasing capacity and willingness to take responsibility for their own learning. By creating classroom environments in which conversations about how and why and in what particular ways we read different texts, these teachers are helping students build "a self-extending system of literacy expertise."[6]

Amy Smith, in describing what appealed to her in the Reading Apprenticeship framework, refers to "the program's support and encouragement of students' taking responsibility for their own learning." In Daniel Moulthrop's classroom, as students learn to take the varied discussion leader roles in reciprocal teaching groups, we see another picture of students' increasing agency and engagement in managing their own comprehension of texts. Students in Lisa Messina and Elizabeth Baker's Academic Literacy classrooms gain independence as they learn to choose, finish, and write about their sustained silent reading books.

Explicit Teaching of Comprehension Strategies in the Context of Meaningful Texts

Providing explicit teaching of comprehension strategies in the context of meaningful texts is another common thread across these classrooms. Carolyn Orta observes, "Teaching reading comprehension is more effective when students apply what they learn to the content materials that they are expected to read and understand."

Lisa Messina and Elizabeth Baker's three-year journey in developing their school's Academic Literacy course underscores the need for teaching reading comprehension strategies in the context of authentic subject-area texts—not only textbooks, but a wide range of texts of science, history, literacy, or mathematics that students at advanced levels of academic literacy need to be able to comprehend, apply, and critique.

Practicing "Smart Routines" to Scaffold Literacy Performance

Another common thread running through the classrooms narratives is the power of "generative" or "smart" routines—routines that students and teachers use regularly that provide practice in high-leverage reading and thinking behaviors and have the capacity to deepen students' understanding over time. Teachers across these chapters are scaffolding students' learning, providing models and guided practice, adding variety, and thinking carefully about pacing and eventual fading of expert support. They work to provide just enough support and just long enough so that progress is constant. Lisa Messina and Elizabeth Baker illustrate this in the way they provide students with increasingly sophisticated prompts over the year as they ask students to write in their sustained silent reading logs. The modeling, discussion, and practice they provide as they introduce each new prompt helps their students develop new abilities while engaging in a familiar routine.

———————

All four of these teacher-authored chapters illustrate the varied ways teachers are incorporating the Reading Apprenticeship framework into their different instructional contexts, increasing their support for students' academic literacy. We invite your exploration of their classroom experiences as inspiration for your own.

2

"A Really Good Conversation"

Engaging Students in Working with Texts

Daniel Moulthrop

Daniel Moulthrop teaches English at San Lorenzo High School in San Lorenzo, California. He has provided leadership for the development of a ninth-grade English course that embeds Academic Literacy in the English curriculum. Here, he describes his introductory unit based on the principles and strategies of Reading for Understanding. *He also incorporates selected readings from* Building Academic Literacy: An Anthology for Reading Apprenticeship. *We learn how he establishes and builds on the foundations of academic literacy early in the course so that his students can acquire the confidence and skills to become better readers.*

———

Five students, three boys and two girls, all ninth graders, have drawn their chairs into a tight circle, photocopies of an excerpt from Luis Rodriguez's *Always Running* in their hands or resting on their knees. One of the students, Donald, keeps looking at a poster on the wall to check the list of reading strategies and suggested kinds of notes he might make on a sticky note to place in the margin. The students are piecing through the first few pages, deciding how much to read before they stop to clarify what they have read, attempt to summarize it, and then discuss what they wonder about it and how they connect to it. Deciding to go page by page, they begin, Jeanette reading the title aloud to the others and then pausing.

"'Always running,'" she repeats, slowly. "I wonder what he's running from."

"Maybe from his past," offers Ricky.

"Nah, he's running from the police," Kenny insists.

James offers another possibility, drawing on the pattern he's noticed in what the class has read recently: "Education. Or no education. Or ignorance."

"I bet we find out. C'mon, let's read," Jeanette tells them, refocusing the group on the text.

And they read. They read to one another, and they listen. After each page, they pause to make sure everyone understands what is happening and to share their questions and ideas. Donald keeps offering the group ideas framed with phrases from the list on the wall, and always loud enough for the teacher to hear. All of them are filling the spaces on the pages with tiny yellow sticky notes, now sticking out all over their pages, with questions like, "Why didn't he ask his teacher?" and comments like, "I've felt that way in class before," or "This seems important," accompanied with arrows pointing to specific text. They are copying each other's notes and questions; they are attempting to answer each other's questions, often by conjecture and sometimes by pointing to something directly in the text. They are having what some of them will later characterize as "a really good conversation about a story."

That does not happen at the beginning of the school year. Some years, it takes longer than others; some years, I even wonder if it will ever happen. But it always does. Eventually, after enough modeling and guided practice, the students become capable of independently navigating, reading, and understanding an unfamiliar text. It always seems like a miracle: these ninth graders—some eager to please, many reticent, most unwilling to characterize themselves as readers, most actively articulating their relationship to books as one of antipathy—somehow become a group of learners who know how to deal with the written word in ways that enable them to make personal connections and ask questions that point to the author's purpose in creating the text. It does not come easily, but Unit 1, Reading Self and Society, provides us with three distinct learning opportunities: to open the conversation about the value of reading in our lives, start metacognitive conversations about how reading happens in our brains, and teach specific strategies that students can use to deepen their comprehension of what they read.

The Context

San Lorenzo High School is in northern California's East Bay, south of Oakland, and across the bay from San Francisco. Our students are, like much of California, an extremely diverse group, representing almost every ethnic group living in the state. We have a large percentage of English language learners and students who qualify for free lunch (both figures between 30 and 40 percent of our student body). Our demographics and test performance make our school comparable to most that are characterized as inner-city or underperforming schools.

Our English department is extremely collegial, planning all courses in teams, and meeting regularly to discuss what students are doing and how we can better support them. Our Academic Literacy course was originally conceived as an interdisciplinary venture, during which the majority of sections were taught by English teachers. But over the course of a three-year pilot, the scheduling difficulties the course presented could not be resolved. Eventually, the English department decided the school would be best served by incorporating the course into the English department and reshaping the course so its goals were those of preparing students for future success in our literature and language arts courses. The Academic Literacy course is eighteen weeks long, and the Reading Self and Society unit is the first unit of the course. (The Academic Literacy course description can be found in Appendix C.)

We focus our curriculum on apprenticing readers to the discipline of English, helping students become metacognitive about what they need to do to read and understand novels, poems, plays, and some expository texts—standard fare for a literature-based language arts classroom. Required by all incoming ninth graders and taught at a twenty-to-one ratio, these fall semester classes are heterogeneous and focus primarily on reading. In the spring semester of the ninth-grade year, all students take a more traditional English class in which they read *Romeo and Juliet* and begin to learn how to write in interpretive, persuasive, descriptive, and reflective modes.

Introducing Reading Self and Society

Our goal of helping students become more self-aware readers is supported in the first semester course by the Reading Self and Society unit, *Building Academic Literacy: An Anthology for Reading Apprenticeship*, and other genre-based units such as the short story, the novel, and poetry. Despite the fact that at our school the Academic Literacy course is essentially an English class, the literacy skills and strategies that we teach are the focus for our faculty's on-site professional development throughout the school year.

The Goals

We have many goals for the Reading Self and Society unit that are very specific about reading and metacognition. Before the end of this unit, we hope that all students will have begun to see themselves as readers, as the writers and subjects of the texts do, and that they also will begin to understand what metacognitive reading and learning looks like, specifically, how to use think-aloud, questioning strategies, summarizing, and personal connection to construct meaning from the texts. Because these are our goals, the texts we choose have two purposes: (1) to give us an opportunity to talk about reading and how or why reading became important to individuals and ourselves and (2) to practice the process of making meaning from the written word.

In my classroom, I use the following pieces from *An Anthology for Reading Apprenticeship*: "Gary Lee," "Kevin Clarke," "Sharon Cho," the excerpt from *The Narrative of the Life of Frederick Douglass*, the excerpt "Learning to Read" from *The Autobiography of Malcolm X*, the poem "Learning to Read" by Frances Harper, an excerpt from *Manchild in the Promised Land* by Claude Brown, and "Silence" by Maxine Hong Kingston from *Woman Warrior*. I also use an excerpt from June Jordan's memoir, *Soldier: A Poet's Childhood*, and excerpts from *Always Running* by Luis Rodriguez. Exhibit 2.1 sets out the first four weeks in this class.

Creating a Sense of Safety

Creating a sense of safety from the beginning is integral to allowing students to grow socially as readers and be able to share their reading practice with one another. I have students interview classmates about books they have read or about their favorite book that was made into a movie (this can be a comic book), and then present what they have learned about each other to the rest of the class. I also have them make name tags for their desks so they will all be able to address one another by name.

On the first or second day of class, students write me an extensive letter in terms of whom they perceive themselves to be as a student, reader, writer, and person. I give them plenty of prompts to help them think through these different facets of their identity—for example:

- When have you felt particularly successful in school?

- When have you been most proud of learning something?

- What's the hardest part about school?

- What do you love to read?

Exhibit 2.1. The First Four Weeks of Daniel Moultrop's Academic Literacy Course

	Week One	Week Two	Week Three	Week Four
Focus	Build safety and community in the classroom Become familiar with classroom routines Introduce goals of the course Introduce metacognition Model good reading behaviors Begin metacognitive conversation practice	Provide opportunities for students to talk about reading, how or why reading became important to individuals and ourselves Introduce useful notation Introduce resource maps Introduce think-aloud process	Introduce "Give One, Get One" Work with more difficult text Build schema Introduce useful questions and question-answer relationships Build a summary	Sort useful questions: Literal questions Interpretative questions Applied questions
Activities	Make name tags for desks Students interview and introduce each other Students write letter about who they are as a reader, a writer, a student, a person	Read with pen and sticky notes in hand Talk to the text—record predictions, questions, connections Draw an image remembered from the text	Sorting questions: "Right There," "Pulling It Together," "Author and Me," "On My Own"	Work in groups—specific roles Reread text passages Orally share responses with each other

	Week One	Week Two	Week Three	Week Four
Readings	Personal reading histories: "Gary Lee" and "Kevin Clarke" interviews	Record favorite language from text Write journal response to "Gary Lee" Excerpt from *The Autobiography of Malcolm X* June Jordan excerpt from *Soldier: A Poet's Childhood*	"Learning to Read" by Frances Harper Excerpt from *The Narrative of the Life of Frederick Douglass* Excerpt from *Woman Warrior* by Maxine Hong Kingston	Excerpt from *Manchild in the Promised Land* by Claude Brown "Sharon Cho" interview Excerpt from *Always Running* by Luis Rodriguez
Reading competencies	Personal dimension Social dimension	Personal dimension Social dimension Cognitive dimension Knowledge-building dimension: Content	Cognitive dimension Knowledge-building dimension: Content and text	Social dimension Cognitive dimension Knowledge-building dimension: Content and text

- What do you hate to read?

- When is reading easy, fun, or particularly difficult for you?

These questions help students begin to think about themselves in these terms. These are the very terms in which I want them to think about themselves for the duration of their high school careers.

We usually start the letter in class, and they finish it for homework. The following day, we do another "interview and introduce" activity around their letter. This helps them become accustomed to working on reading in the social dimension. It also affirms their identities as students and participants in the class and reinforces learning classmates' names. This interview format permits students to retain some control over how they represent themselves to others.

Developing Metacognition

In these first days of the course, I introduce students to the major goals of the course. I do this by starting with the word *metacognition,* which I write large on the board. I ask them all to say it out loud, in unison, so they hear themselves using it.

I want them eventually to be able to speak fluently about metacognition. I talk about all the goals of the course—unit by unit, skill by skill, strategy by strategy—relating them all to the idea of metacognition. I explain how each goal is essentially about getting us all to think more about our thinking so that we can become conscious of how we read and how we can read more effectively.

Reading "Gary Lee"

Within the first week, the students know most of their classmates' names, know my name, have their instructional materials, and are beginning to understand the goals of the course, so I move ahead to the interview with Gary Lee in *Building Academic Literacy: An Anthology for Reading Apprenticeship* (see Exhibit 2.2). Gary Lee is a young man in an adult literacy class who is finally learning how to read fifteen years after graduating from high school. Because this interview reads almost like the spoken word, it is immediately accessible to almost all the students. In addition, it presents issues of illiteracy and injustice in the classroom, and so it immediately engages some of the more reluctant readers.

From the very beginning, I tell students they must read with a pen or pencil in hand as well as a pad of small sticky notes. First, I ask the students to *skim* the reading and note what pops out at them on a sticky note. I tell them, for example, that they might make predictions about what the piece will be about, or they may write questions about unfamiliar words or ideas. This is a way for me to familiarize them with what will become crucial tasks in future classes. We talk about the questions or predictions they wrote down, but right now, I'm not expecting anything huge or monumental. They are just becoming familiar with hearing their own voices in the classroom and responding to my instruction.

What Makes a Good Reader

I explain that I will read aloud to them now, but in the coming weeks, they will begin to take on more and more of the responsibility for reading to and with their classmates. I read the background information on Gary Lee to them and then read the first sentence: "Schools are big factories." I stop right there to tell them I have a question: How are schools like big factories? We talk about what Gary might mean by this: that there are a lot of people involved, and that factories have products, so the products of a school might be its students. I then tell them my prediction that Gary Lee will give us examples of the ways schools are like factories. I also tell them that making a prediction about what is coming up is a step all good readers take: that we are constantly making predictions and checking them against what we read.

★ Schema

★ Questions

★ Suggestions

★ Comments/Opinions

★ Metacognitive stuff

A cnxNs

★ Predictions

★ Clarifying Questions

Why did I take that class?

What does he mean by that?

Dang, I can't believe that!

Go Back to School!!

P.1

GARY LEE

"The world is set up to where you've got to read and write to be able to function in it. It's really frustrating if you can't, and you beat up on yourself a lot," says Gary Lee, who is now learning how to read, fifteen years after receiving his high school diploma. He and two other students from his adult literacy class have written and produced a play that dramatizes the frustration and limitations of life without literacy.

Schools are big factories. When you're a little kid, you're the raw material, and when you get to the end, they spit you out. Somewhere in between, if you don't keep up, you get chucked off into the reject pile. That's basically what happened to me.

That's True

Reading has been a problem with me ever since I was a little kid. I went to three or four elementary schools. Before I even got to junior high, they put me into a special ed. class and that was what I would call the reject pile.

My mom and dad got a divorce when I was what? Seven years old? My mom was a waitress and was trying to raise two kids. She could read pretty good, but she wasn't a very advanced reader or anything. I went through a couple junior high schools and then I went to two different high schools. I guess I just got lost in the changes.

Why are you always moving?

I know some people like that.

My mom, she never really stressed to me to go to school and learn stuff. She just said, "Go to school." So I went to school. But when I was in high school, the teachers would never make me do anything. I would go to class and they would say, "Well, you showed up, I'll give you a 'D.'" So I would go to school, but it was basically a big joke.

What kind teacher is that?

That's why Mr. H doesn't gives D's.

Nadine Rosenthal, SPEAKING OF READING

Gary Lee

One teacher was real nice to me and helped me out, but then I moved again. I had to meet new friends, a whole new set of teachers. I guess some people don't realize that moving around really hurts a kid. As soon as you settle down and get used to the new set of teachers and friends, your family moves and you don't have any control over it.

That Must be such.

One time in the shuffle, they got my papers screwed up and they injected me into a regular high school format. I went up to this one teacher and told her, "I can't read. I can't do this." They put me into the special ed. class, where we played cards. For two years. But they gave me a high school diploma at the end. Yeah, it's not worth the ink it's printed on. I didn't even care when I got it. I could have left school in the sixth grade.

I am good at sports.

No one in school ever tried to figure out what I was really talented at. The only thing they spent a lot of time figuring out was what I *wasn't* talented at. Nobody cared what I was interested in. Nobody ever tried to figure out what I could do and try to build off of that.

Everybody is talented.

In the fifteen or so years since high school, I haven't done much. I like going to car races and I guess that's why I started learning to read. I read a lot of car magazines, although when I first started reading them, I was lousy at it. I would just sit down and try to read them as best I could. The words are fairly simple. Those were the only kind of magazines I would read because it was something I was interested in—I wanted to learn about the racing cars.

That's good that you are interested in cars.

Then a couple of years ago I went to the literacy program because I was mad at myself. I was still running from this reading thing. I wanted to progress in my life and I knew I had to learn to read and write to do it. I looked in the front of the *Yellow Pages* where there's a lot of community services listed. The first time I went to the literacy program, it

Why run?

Exhibit 2.2. Laying the Groundwork for Talking to the Text: The "Gary Lee" Piece

felt like I was going to the dentist. I didn't know what to expect. They gave me a couple tests and then they gave me a tutor. They don't have a magical wand or anything. They couldn't just crack me in the head and make me able to read and write.

I had one tutor for a couple of years, but then she went on to something different, I guess. Now I've got another one and she's very organized. She even makes me more organized because she makes me put down what time I study and what I study at what time. I like that. She tutors me for three hours and then she gives me six hours of homework. It really doesn't make my social life too great, but I do most of it anyway. The harder that I push, the farther I go. I don't want to be doing this for eight years.

I came up with this idea that I wanted to write a play about what it was like to not read and write. It's funny because I had never, ever been to a play, and I've never attempted to write one, and I've never attempted acting. It just popped into my head one day. I got together with two other students who were willing to go out on a limb with me. So we sat down and worked for about a year discussing our own personal trials on reading and what we could say out of it all. We sat down and wrote it and produced it and did most of the work ourselves.

We acted out parts of our three stories. My story was about when I got pulled from a regular school and got bussed around town to a special ed. class where the teacher was totally mean to me. She would always grab a hold of my ear and yank on it if I wasn't doing stuff right, or if she was frustrated at me or just was having a bad day. The second scene was about when one of the other students was in high school. I played the teacher and he played himself. The teacher tried to make him stand up in class and read, but he couldn't read and we showed the frustration in that. And the third scene is about when the third student is in high school and she goes to a counselor and he tells her that she doesn't have the ability to even learn how to read.

The play goes from grade school to high school and the very last scene is where the other male student goes to get a job and he can't fill out the application or run a computer because he doesn't know how to read so he's turned down for the job. We're putting the play on all around the area. There's a part in the play that goes something like, "I'm bound by invisible chains, but one of these days, I'm going to get rid of these chains that have bound me." People walk away from the play real sad. I guess that's what we wanted them to do, but I was surprised when I saw some people in the audience crying. But we make them laugh, too.

I used to think that I couldn't do anything, but now I think things are open to me pretty much. Believing in myself is a lot of it. In school all they taught me was, "You're not going to amount to anything."

You're lousy at this, and you will always be lousy." Now I know I ain't the greatest, but if I work hard, I will overcome all of this. I want to be the first one in my family to learn to read and write to a high level. Then I want to go back to school and open my own business.

I know it's going to be a long haul. Learning to read takes time. But over time you get more familiar with it and it starts to become easier for you. It's like the first time I went skiing. I was falling all over the place. I was the lousiest skier in the world. But now that I've done it for a few years, I've gotten pretty good at it. The first time I went skiing, there was a tiny hump and I couldn't get up over it. Now a little hump like that would be nothing to me.

Exhibit 2.2. *continued*

I tell the students that I want them to behave like good readers: readers who ask questions, try to make connections between what they are reading and what they already know, make predictions about what they read, and check the accuracy of their predictions as they go along. At many points during the course, we will have conversations about what makes a good reader, but right now, I am just beginning to model good reading practices for them. Later, when they have become familiar enough with what good reading is like, they will be better prepared for that conversation.

Note Taking and Journal Response

I repeatedly encourage the students to follow along in their text as I read and use their sticky notes to record their predictions, questions, and connections. Connections between what they are reading and what they already know are often the easiest to notice and one of the key skills needed to make sense of the text and provide motivation to continue reading.

After the first paragraph, we pause to check my prediction about schools and factories. We talk about what Gary might mean by the "reject pile" and make more predictions about what Gary will tell us next, and I ask them to write down their predictions. By the end of the semester, I want all my students to be able to make these predictions, connections, and questions automatically, without any prompting from me. The goal now is to become familiar with the process of noticing what is happening in our brains and writing it down.

We continue reading together, with them following as I read aloud from the piece. After four or five paragraphs, after Gary has described what school was like for him, we pause to share what we have been recording. Typically, some of the students have not written anything, so I ask them to take a minute to reread the first few paragraphs and jot down any connections or responses to what they read. We read through the rest of the piece together, pausing for questions, clarifications, predictions, or meaningful personal connections.

At the end, I ask them to read back through the piece silently and find the one sentence or short passage that really speaks to them or that they think might be the most important moment in the text. We share these, with the explicit caveat that more than one person may choose the same sentence. Hearing a passage repeated reinforces its importance for us as a group.

One student wrote:

> "It's frustrating if you can't read and you beat up on yourself a lot." I choose this sentence for my powerful moment because I was stunned and couldn't believe what it said. For one thing how did he get his high school diploma if he couldn't read, it's crazy. Why couldn't he read, he must be very lazy, and/or very erisponsible.

We talk about the meanings of these important moments. I ask students what they find to be important about the sentence they chose or the sentence they just heard a classmate read. By sharing the parts of the piece with which they connected, students begin to see how personal the experience of reading is. Sharing those parts and saying, "I really liked the part when . . .," or "When he said . . . , I felt . . .," is a practice that good readers are always engaging in through internal conversation or talk with other readers.
Sharing connections also provides an opportunity for students to practice verbally what they will later do in writing, with their independent reading logs, in interpretive essays in future courses, and in their homework for tonight.

After sharing, I ask them to copy the passage they chose at the top of a blank piece of paper, along with their name and the date. Journals are on loose-leaf paper so that I can read and respond to them as quickly as possible. This becomes their homework: a one-page journal response to Gary Lee, focusing on their chosen passage and its meaning for them and for Gary. I tell them we will share the journals the following day, so they should not write anything they do not want to share. I also tell them that we will write journals in this class for many purposes: sometimes as responses to what we read, sometimes to try to get inside what we are reading, and sometimes to reflect on our own learning, our reading practice, or our work. Tonight's journal is a simple response to what they have read. In this assignment, one student wrote:

> I like the quote, "The harder I push the farther I go."
> That's a good quote for me because it's the reason why I
> get good grades now. My mom pushes me to get better
> than a "C" in everything by making consequences if I
> don't. And now I'm old enough to understand that.

Useful Notation

The next day, we start off sharing journals with each other. Here is where I introduce the system of useful notation I learned from my colleagues: the four common symbols for comments when responding to writing that are set out in Exhibit 2.3.

I randomly distribute a journal page and tell the students they must read and respond to the journal responses of at least three of their classmates using the system of useful notation I explain to them and recording any other comments they might have; they initial the bottom of the page to indicate they have read it. I also ask them to share aloud with the rest of the class anything they read that particularly struck them (I usually have to model this behavior for the first few weeks). After five or six minutes of reading one another's work, we debrief, sharing what seems important about the journals and the role of reading in our lives. Five or six minutes may seem short, but for the first shared journal, they may not have written a lot, or I may be worried that they will start veering off task if their time is not directed. If they are engaged and on task, I might extend the time.

✳	I like the way you said this.
☺	I agree with what you have written.
?	I don't understand what you are trying to communicate.
📦	This idea is in a box; unpack it! (Elaborate on it.)

Exhibit 2.3. Useful Notation for Responding to Journals

Resource Maps and the Think-Aloud Process

The major goal for the next few days uses the excerpt from Malcolm X's autobiography in *Building Academic Literacy: An Anthology for Reading Apprenticeship*: identifying what motivates Malcolm X to read and what kind of connections we as readers can make to that motivation. The reading happens much as it did when we read "Gary Lee": slowly, with ongoing textual interaction and pauses to clarify, model my thought processes, and elicit from students information about what is happening in their brains. We read most of the excerpt together, though I may have the students try to read portions quietly or in groups.

After we have finished reading the selection, I introduce the students to a structured system of note making in which they build what we call *resource maps*. Resource maps are visually organized notes about important themes, language, images, ideas, and moments from the text.[1] The maps provide a structure that enables students to track important elements of the text. The maps themselves are not essential; many other types of graphic organizers can serve the same or similar purposes. As with many other graphic organizing structures, the maps can be adapted for all sorts of texts. With the Malcolm X excerpt, I have students track and focus on motivation to read, obstacles to success, and strategies for overcoming obstacles. I also have them record significant background information provided to them about Malcolm X. Exhibit 2.4 provides an example of a resource map for the Malcolm X reading.

The most important information the students track has to do with themselves and their reading processes. Parts of the resource maps have headings prompting students to become aware of their own connections to the text:

"Background Information"

"Favorite Language"

"Motivation"

"Metacognitive Me"

"Obstacles/Strategies"

"Questions/Possible Topic for My Journal"

These headings ask students to notice what they are enjoying about the text, what questions the reading elicits, and what is happening in their brains as they read—in other words, what strategies they use to make sense of the text.

We go back through the text, piecing together a kind of metanarrative or renarrative about what motivates Malcolm X to read and how he overcomes his lack of education. I ask questions like, "Which moments do you remember? What images are stuck in your head? What do those images tell us about Malcolm X's struggle to read?" and "Why is this part confusing? What did you do to make it less confusing? How did you figure it out?" Every moment is an opportunity for us to discuss where on the map we record the information—a process of building a schema about literacy that we will draw on later in the course. We also allow ourselves a great deal of time to talk about our own personal enjoyment of the text—the salient images, the words that stick with us—because the level of enjoying a text can be a integral source of motivation in a literature-focused classroom.

The discussion and note-making prompting continue until the students have filled their maps with words, notes, and questions, quoted passages as well as pictures, charting their deeper understanding of the excerpt. In one part of the map, I ask students to spend five minutes drawing a picture of a powerful image they remember from the excerpt. It does not have to be great art, I tell them, just their own best effort to record what they saw in their heads. My own stick figure representation of Malcolm X reading in his jail cell convinces them that I am not expecting beautiful illustrations.

When the resource maps are finished, the students have variously recorded under "Obstacles/Strategies" Malcolm X's lack of education, along with the fact that he was in prison, and quotations that illustrate his frustration, such as his feeling that the words "might as well have been in Chinese." Under "Motivation," they have recorded information and quotations about the freedom he found in books, his pride in initial success, his increased sensitivity to issues of racism, and his desire to learn the truth and to emulate his friend Bimbi, whose "stock of knowledge" made him envious. The students also record their favorite language in the piece and share those moments with one another. After I can see that all the students understand both the piece and the way we are discussing it and making notes, I make sure to close with some sort of "meta-discussion" about how much more we have understood as a result of our discussion—how we have not just read but constructed a deeper understanding of Malcolm X's life and struggles with literacy.

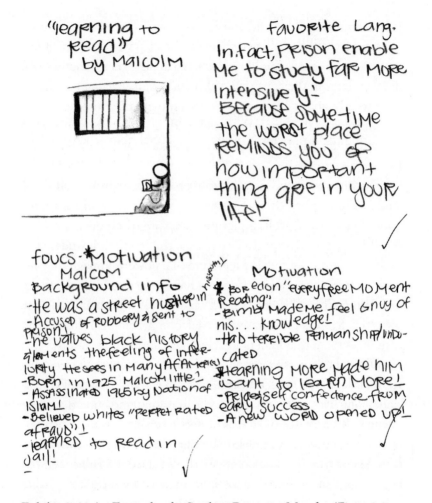

Exhibit 2.4. An Example of a Student Resource Map for "Learning to Read," by Malcolm X

Introducing the Think-Aloud Process

By now, we are well into the second week of school, a good time to introduce think-aloud, a process that helps students practice the mental activities or strategies engaged in by good readers. It helps them focus on comprehension, and it helps the teacher know when

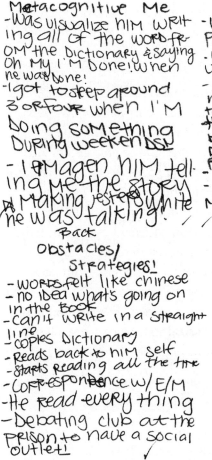

Metacognitive Me
-Was visualize him writing all of the words from the Dictionary & saying Oh my I'm Done! when he was Done!
-I got to sleep around 3 or four when I'm Doing something During weekends!
-I imagen him telling me the story & Making jestors while he was talking! /
Back
Obstacles/
Strategies!
-words felt like chinese
-no idea what's going on in the book
-Can't write in a straight line
-copies Dictionary
-Reads back to him self
-Starts reading all the time
-Correspondence w/E/M
-He read every thing
-Debating club at the Prison to have a social outlet! ✓

question/Journal
-why Do people pretent to read!
-What would you use your time at prison
-How did his life changed after he larned to read
-How would your life be differrent if you Didn't know how to read!
-literacy & lifes optios
-Value of home Made education.

④

Oun lopez

Exhibit 2.4. *continued*

and how students' comprehension goes awry. I use a June Jordan
piece for this, a poem from *Soldier: A Poet's Childhood*, but we start
with other texts for which think-aloud is much easier.

I explain exactly why we are thinking aloud: because reading is
a mental process, it requires thinking, and part of what the students

will learn in this class is how to pay attention to their thinking. We will not always be thinking aloud, I tell them, but at this stage, we must do everything we can to notice what is happening in our heads so we can find out what we are already doing and what we need to learn to do. Later, these processes will become a part of what we do on paper when we read.

We model the process with Play-Doh, with the students building animals from Play-Doh and thinking aloud the steps as they do this. Before moving on to June Jordan's poem, we begin with an easy or familiar text, for example, the Pledge of Allegiance or song lyrics my students know. I ask the students to read silently, to slow themselves down, and share with the class as much of what is happening in their heads as they can. When they start, they often talk about what they want for lunch or what they are going to do after school.

Using Problem-Solving Strategies

As they progress into reading the texts with a partner, I begin to hear some students articulating questions or connections they are making. One partner reads and thinks aloud while the other listens. After each partner has had a chance to read and think aloud, we talk generally about what they are noticing is happening in their own and their partners' minds. In the context of these conversations, I encourage them toward the meaning-making mental behavior that helps them understand what they read.

After we are done, I ask them to reflect on the activity, responding to the following prompts:

- What is thinking aloud?

- What do you have to do in order to do it well?

- How did you feel as you were sharing your thoughts with your partner?

- What was easy or difficult for you?

- What will you try to do better next time?

We share these reflections with each other, building a list on the overhead or board to record what good thinking aloud looks like.

Asking Questions, Finding Answers

Now that we have read a few pieces, logged some success, built some confidence, and begun to understand what happens in our brains as we read, we are ready to tackle one of the more difficult pieces. I like to use writing by Frederick Douglass, not only because he should be read by every American but also because he touches on themes that students will recognize from the Malcolm X excerpt.

I prepare students for the challenge in a few ways. To activate and generate more schema for understanding the piece, we do a "Give One, Get One" on the subject of slavery in America. This collaborative activity draws on the content knowledge, ideas, and experience students already have regarding the topic. I introduce "Give One, Get One" as it is discussed in *Reading for Understanding* (p. 103), modeling not only the kind of information they should write down on the "Give One" side—as much as they know and are reasonably confident is true—but also how I want them to record information from others—by talking to each other, not just copying information, and recording the name of the classmate who provided the information. I give them two minutes to write down what they know. Then they have five minutes to get as much information as they can. I participate too, exchanging facts and knowledge and writing down everyone's name next to the information provided, praising students for their knowledge and for following instructions and for gathering lots of information.

After five minutes of this activity, each person shares one fact he or she learned from a classmate, then the classmate cited shares next, and so on, creating a chain of knowledge. This activity both validates their prior knowledge and helps them practice participating in class and speaking to their classmates.

By this point, the students feel secure that they know more about slavery than they thought they did. Sometimes I use the Francis Harper poem "Learning to Read" to lead into the Frederick Douglass excerpt. This poem provides an opportunity to build more schema and practice reading a slightly different (but in some ways more accessible) genre. The goal is to identify Harper's purpose, which is to show the link between illiteracy and power—specifically, the power to enslave. We read the poem in the way I want them to read poetry all the time: multiple times, quietly and aloud, and with a pen in hand, writing notes about their own ideas, questions, wonderings, and the emerging themes they notice. Before we start to read, we brainstorm the kinds of comments and questions they might write as they read. I then ask them to scan the poem quietly, writing down initial responses (words they do not know, connections, and so forth).

We share those connections, and then we listen to ourselves reading the poem. I read the poem first to model how I want them to read: slowly and without stopping at the ends of the lines. This way, too, they hear me pronouncing any words they are not sure how to pronounce.

Before we begin to talk about the poem, we read it again, perhaps with each student reading a stanza or one or two volunteers reading the whole poem.

Discussing the poem is fairly straightforward. I ask the students for the questions they have (these might be written down or just simmering in their heads), reminding them that our goal is to identify why Frances Harper wrote the poem. Then we use their questions to get to the essence of the poem. Because this is a new process for the students, they do not always have the best questions. They sometimes ask, "How old was Frances Harper when she wrote this?" or "Did she have brothers or sisters?" or "Who is Mr. Turner?"

Although these questions do demonstrate an interest on the students' part, they do not help us understand what we are reading. I encourage them toward other kinds of questions by giving them examples of the kinds of questions that will help us understand the poem, for example, "Why doesn't knowledge agree with slavery?" or "What does it mean to 'steal a little from the book'?" I point out that useful questions focus on the language used and its purpose, and then I encourage them to give me more questions, heaping on the praise for valiant attempts and helping them shape their questions to make them more useful.

I want to hear their questions and help them see the power they have to help us understand what they read. I explicitly articulate that to them.

Reading Together in Groups

When we get to The Frederick Douglass piece, I arrange tables in heterogeneous groups of four because the students will be reading together. I tell them that this will be difficult reading, but because they have the skills to do this and they will be working in groups, they will not have to figure out what to do all on their own.

Before we begin, we make a list on the board of all the resources they have to help them understand what they are doing. I remind them to use their sticky notes to write notes about connections, predictions, questions, and anything else happening in their brains. I remind them that reading is a mental process and that sometimes they will have to talk about what they are reading to understand what is going on. I also tell them that after we read, we will go back through the excerpt to make graphic organizers of what we have understood about Douglass.

I read the first paragraph aloud to the class, modeling all my thinking at the end, and eliciting questions and deeper understandings from them. With that, I tell them, they are ready to read the rest themselves. I give them a minute to organize themselves, and then I start to circulate around the classroom to listen and help out as needed. The groups may choose to read silently or out loud, each student taking a turn or one student alone. After about ten minutes, I call the class's attention back together, and we debrief a little about the issues that are arising, points that need clarification, and the progress they are making. Then they continue working, which may take the rest of the class period. This part is the most difficult reading in the unit, so I give them enough time to do it well.

We again use resource maps as a way to explore the excerpt and the ways power is represented—both the power in the owner-slave relationship and the power Douglass gains from learning to read. Because this is such a difficult excerpt, one of the first tasks is building a summary of what we have read. This first exposure to summarizing requires that we spend some time talking about what a summary is and the differences between main ideas and details. This summary will probably be a simple, bulleted list of important events, so we do not have to delve into the teaching of writing summaries.

The goal of the summary is to recognize and catalogue main ideas and events. When we encounter any moment in Douglass's life that we recognize as an obstacle, we record it under the heading of obstacles as well as in the summary. We continue to pay attention to motivation, the counterbalance to the obstacles. Often students have deeper questions—some that we can answer and some we cannot. As with the Malcolm X piece, I ask them to record their questions. In general, we build our organizers about Douglass just as we did with Malcolm X.

Their completed maps will have images, records of their favorite language and how they made meaning from the text, moments that revealed motivation or obstacles, and their own questions about the text. I strive to make the note making multimodal, giving them chances to draw, talk to one another, write, and listen. This note-making process has to be thoroughly thought through. Before we begin, I make sure I know what I want every student to have written on their maps, as well as what points they might record in notes about their individual exploration of the text.

The Question-Answer Relationship

Once most of the basic structures of our class have been set up, I introduce the notion of the question-answer relationship so they can begin to recognize effective questions and learn how to formulate them. Asking good questions and understanding how they are answered is an important literacy skill.

I have the students each write two or three of their most interesting questions (ones they have recorded earlier as notes stuck to the text or on their resource maps) large and legibly on a half-sheet of paper, which they tape to the wall or the board. Then, as a whole class or in small groups, I ask them to sort the questions into categories based not on the content of the question but on the steps they would have to take to reach the answers. This is a little confusing, so I may give them examples of questions based on recent or familiar movies and explain how we might have to go about answering them.

What I'm looking for, of course, are the following categories of questions:

"Right There," a question whose answer is right there in the text. All the reader has to do is copy it down or repeat it.

"Pulling It Together," a question whose answer is in the text, but the reader has to pull it together from different parts of the text. He or she cannot simply copy it from one place.

"Author and Me," a question whose answer is not in the text. The reader has to use the information provided in the text and his or her own schema to figure out the answer.

"On My Own," a question whose answer is not in the text. The reader does not have to have read the text to answer the question, but reading the text will inform his or her answer.

I have practiced this as both a whole-class, question-by-question, teacher-led process and as a loosely structured activity in which the students are doing most of the talking and figuring and I provide only a few well-placed prompts or clues. If the students are capable of running most of the activity, I typically lead the class in some adjusting of categories and resorting of questions to direct them to where they make the most sense. I also teach them other names for these categories—names for question types that are used more commonly at my school: "Literal Questions" for "Right There" and "Pulling It Together," "Interpretive Questions" for "Author and Me," and "Applied Questions" for "On My Own" questions. I also explain the meaning of these terms (what it means to *interpret* a text, for instance, or how we might *apply* a theme from a text to our own lives).

Reading for Homework

At this point in the course, the students usually are able to succeed at reading for homework. Before they do this, we have an explicit conversation about all they have learned and about the differences between reading at home and reading in school. We talk about everything they will need to be successful readers on their own at home, along with the kinds of reading and comprehension strategies they will use when they encounter an obstacle.

The first text they read at home is the "Sharon Cho" piece about a young woman inspired by comic book heroes. Toward the end of class, we do some prereading, discussing some of the books that have been meaningful to us and the lessons we can learn from them, and we read the first paragraph or so of "Sharon Cho" together. I ask them to read at home as we read in school, with a pencil in their hand and sticky notes at their side, writing down their responses, connections, questions, and wonderings. I tell them that I will look at their homework readings to see how well they were able to make notes and be metacognitive.

Developing Reader Confidence

With the Luis Rodriguez excerpt from *Always Running*, I have students read in groups in class. I assign each group a different reading focus that will then become the basis of a short presentation the group members give to their classmates on the following subjects: the author's purpose, important biographical information, what reading means to Luis Rodriguez, and major obstacles to reading and how he overcame them. I tell them they are responsible for reading and understanding the whole piece but that each group will create posters and short presentations that examine the reading with their particular focus. The posters should include important information and interpretations of what they have read, as well as several direct quotations from the text that support what they believe they have found out about Luis Rodriguez. The activity requires students to talk to one another and work in the social dimension of reading, and it demonstrates the importance of keeping a reading goal in mind, for different goals produce different results.

Final Assessment: Becoming Readers

Our final assessment, about a week long, for the Reading Self and Society unit is a role-playing activity in which the students take on the part of one of the authors they have read and argue to a mock school board the importance of books and of reading. Students often seem resistant to role-playing, but they eventually catch on and realize how much fun they can have. I provide them with a list of questions to consider having to do with why reading is important and the value of books and literacy in our world today. Helping them understand my expectations often seems to require a lot of repetition and explicit instruction: "Yes, you will pretend you are Luis Rodriguez, and then answer the questions. Yes, you will have to reread the Luis Rodriguez article to do this." I also include two nonauthor roles to fill out the cast of characters: a teacher representative and a student representative, providing voices more specific to our community.

I organize the class into two groups and have them decide who will take on which role. This is usually a loud and argumentative activity, but they are doing what I have asked them to do, and sometimes life is loud and argumentative. Each group chooses a captain and recorder—to facilitate the decision-making process and make a final list of the role that each student is taking. They clamor for the teacher and student positions, so it is best to make sure they understand the special requirements of those roles: that the student role-playing a teacher is to interview at least three different teachers, while the student in the student role will interview three different students. Each role player will synthesize what he or she learns from the interviewees about books and reading.

Once the roles are decided, students make a name tag, starting to take ownership of their role. Then they reread the article or complete their interview and prepare their responses. While they reread, I have them keep the questions about reading in mind as they start to make notes about possible answers, helping them move to preparing responses. Homework for that night can be to finish interviews or the first draft of responses.

Over the next two days, along with whatever else is happening in class, the students share responses with one another and see how they sound. Students also do a run-through with me, and I provide each one feedback in the form of a chart listing "What you're doing well" and "What you need to work on." The teacher run-through is a big motivator because the students often realize how unprepared they are.

When I think they are ready, I have them prepare comments on note cards. Toward the end of the day before the presentations, I distribute the "Questions from the Board" handout. The students assign one another responsibility for asking specific questions from the first handout, and they also brainstorm more relevant questions so everyone will have two questions prepared to ask the panelists.

Homework the night before the presentation is to practice both alone and in front of another person.

During the mock school board meeting, each group takes a turn at being the panel of reading experts and the board. I arrange the classroom to look like a board meeting, and I set the tone by striving for a feeling of professionalism combined with a sense of humor. At the start, the students sit down in their groups, one as the panel, one as the board, and I give them five minutes to collect themselves and make sure they have everything they need: their note cards and any other props they might have brought (some students bring a book or dress in character). The board picks a chairperson to lead discussion and determine the order of questions and procedures for how responses will be taken. I also give the board a note-taking organizer and explain to them how to fill it out. Then I welcome everyone to the board meeting and see what happens.

Sometimes students who have been quiet or uninvolved for the past three weeks suddenly come out of their shells, speaking in Malcolm X's preacherly tones, with Frederick Douglass's intellectual diction, or emulating Luis Rodriguez's *barrio* slang. Watching this transformation is one of my favorite moments in the unit.

Concluding the Unit

To conclude the unit, I often have students write a metacognitive and reflective letter to me about how they think they did on the panel presentation and what they have learned since the beginning of the course. I ask them to reflect on the kind of reader they were at the beginning and the kind of a reader they are now, what motivates them to read, what obstacles they routinely face, and what strategies they now use to overcome those roadblocks. We do this sort of reflection throughout the course, and they did a similar one for me the first day of class, and I remind them of what they have written on these occasions.

Reading over these reflections helps me understand not only which parts of the unit are working well for which students but also where I should focus my energy in the next units. In my responses to my students' reflections, I comment on the growth that I have seen in them and the opportunities they have for future growth.

Conclusion

Some students, other teachers, and parents complain to me that much of the metacognitive approach I use is unnecessary. They ask, "What if a student doesn't need all of that? What if I just get what I'm reading? Why should I have to explain everything that's going on in my head? Isn't that a distraction from all the stuff I'm supposed to be learning?" Although those questions are important and they certainly point to the frustrations experienced by some of the students in the upper academic echelons, they miss the point. Of course, there is content to deliver, but the most important goal of this course is to help students become aware of themselves as readers who are doing real intellectual work every time they look at a written text, a sign on a wall, or a movie. The point is that our brains are on and working, and in talking about the work, our brains are doing work. In being metacognitive about our reading processes, even the student who "gets it" now understands *how* she got it and can help others by modeling her own expert reading practice.

In the end, understanding the content and the processes used for gaining that understanding enable students to have a good conversation about a story. This is not an easy skill to acquire. A good conversation about a text requires students to listen to each other, be aware of their own questions, have a desire to explore answers to one another's questions, return to the text for clarification, and relate what they are reading to their own lives. A good conversation requires readers to care about what they are reading, and caring is possible only if readers feel they have some hope of understanding the text and some degree of confidence derived from their own reading and past successes.

Awakening the Reader Within

Lisa Messina, Elizabeth Baker

Lisa Messina is in her seventh year of teaching at Jefferson High School in Daly City, California. For the past three years, she has taught Academic Literacy and Advanced Placement (AP) language and composition. Elizabeth Baker is beginning her fourth year of teaching at Jefferson; this is her second year as the Academic Literacy coordinator. Both teachers work with the whole staff as literacy coaches to facilitate their school's mission of improving literacy across the curriculum. In this chapter, they describe their journey in creating an Academic Literacy course and outline the first unit of that course, "Who Am I as a Reader?" which establishes the routines and builds the foundation for their work on reading throughout the year.

N ever doubt that a small group of thoughtful, committed people can change the world. Indeed, it is the only thing that ever has." This quotation from Margaret Mead hangs in both of our classrooms, reminding us that all of the hard work we have put into students' reading improvement matters.

Four years ago, as members of a group of seven teachers from Jefferson High School, we set out to change the world and to fight for an Academic Literacy class to help struggling readers succeed. Our intentions were honorable, although our training was limited. We read the professional literature, including the description of the

Academic Literacy class in *Reading for Understanding*; we attended workshops; we hired a reading specialist; and we made political enemies by eliminating the freshman elective and replacing it with an Academic Literacy class.

Jefferson High School is a school of twelve hundred students just south of San Francisco. Our student population is diverse, reflecting that of the San Francisco Bay Area. Seventy percent of students come from families in which English is not the first language, and the majority of our students were not born in the United States, immigrating from over thirty countries.

The Journey: Creating an Academic Literacy Course

In the spring of 1999, acknowledging the need to give students a strong literacy foundation at the beginning of high school, the administration and faculty of our school agreed to create a two-period block of English and Academic Literacy for ninth-grade students. We were able to use Title I funds to set the enrollment limit in this block at twenty rather than the usual thirty-five students in most classes at Jefferson. Although we started the Academic Literacy course by tracking students into high and lower classes, we found that heterogeneous classes benefit all students. Some students enter Academic Literacy reading at the second- or third-grade level, and others are planning to take AP English in their junior year. The nature of reading is such that even if all students are at the same reading level according to a reading assessment, their strengths, weaknesses, and motivations related to reading vary greatly. In an Academic Literacy class, this variability can be a resource rather than an impediment to students' reading growth.

Year One of Academic Literacy

In planning our first Academic Literacy course, we created a chart of strategies that good readers use, such as predicting and summarizing, and in the beginning weeks of the new year, we handed the chart to our students. *Memorize these strategies and do them*, we said. *This will make you a better reader.*

Over the course of the first quarter, we tested and retested the students on their ability to identify no fewer than thirty strategies. Many students memorized the names of these valuable tools. But at the end of the first quarter, when we asked students to demonstrate their ability to use strategies like questioning or making connections, few of them showed any authentic use of these tools.

Most students would simply read straight through the paragraph, never stopping, never questioning their comprehension, never indicating in any way that reading was a process. We had given them a tool belt but had failed to explain how to use the tools or measure them for correct size. We *had* succeeded in creating classroom environments in which students were engaged with self-selected texts at their independent reading levels and were aware that there are strategies that can be used to tackle difficult texts. Students read a lot, talked about books, and even practiced keeping reading logs. But we felt we had failed to help students connect the strategies we had taught them to their individual struggles with reading.

In June, at the end of our first year of Academic Literacy, we met with the other Academic Literacy teachers, as we had faithfully done throughout the year and the previous summer, to discuss our students' progress. True, many students had read more in that one year than they had in their entire lives. Many students could list strategies that good readers use. Even more interesting, many students who had been considered poor readers at the beginning of the year believed that they were "good" readers now. Nevertheless, many teachers talked about their frustration with students' limited comprehension and limited ability to apply reading strategies to texts outside of the ones they used for "practicing strategies."

In their final papers, a reflective reading letter, students wrote enthusiastically about how each of us had taught them to read, how we were the most fabulous reading teachers they had ever had, and how much they had improved. What students did *not* include in their letters was a convincing analysis of how they had changed as readers or insights into specific ways that strategies helped them comprehend difficult text. We had begun the process of making these students more literate and more fluent with books at their independent level, but we wondered if they could apply the strategies they had learned to their difficult science text. We knew that students' increased motivation and positive identity as readers were crucial building blocks for engaging in critical academic reading, but we saw little evidence that students could see the connections between questioning and making meaning or navigate the difficult readings they must access in social studies.

We had accomplished our first goal: to foster a love of reading—or at least to create an interest in reading. We are very proud of the students who read ten or fifteen or even twenty books that year, but most of these books were at their independent reading level and all of them were narrative. Although one of the major goals of the class is to build fluency with these texts, we were creating students who were better readers in only one world: the world of free choice and narrative texts. In our experience, students enter high school knowing a great deal about narrative text structure. Thus, we had accomplished a crucial but relatively easy task. By not helping students use their new-found confidence as readers to help them tackle challenging academic text, we had failed to reach the most important goal of assisting these students to become "engaged, fluent, and competent readers of both academic and recreational texts."[1] We had failed to incorporate the "academic" aspect of Academic Literacy into the course. The staff of Jefferson High School expected us to help students make sense of challenging, expository text, and we simply had not done that. In fact, this remains the most challenging aspect of our curriculum three years later.

Year Two of Academic Literacy

Although we had to deal with many of the drawbacks of public education, such as teacher turnover, we made some major strides in year two of Academic Literacy. We decided to focus on two aspects of the curriculum: metacognition and expository text. Most important, we realized that this class would be effective only if we individualized the program by working with students to uncover their strengths, weaknesses, and goals in regard to literacy. We asked students to read difficult text and explain the "process" they used to understand—or attempt to understand—it. We dipped our toes in the ocean of think-aloud as well, making the invisible process of reading visible by verbalizing our thinking and problem-solving process as we read, mainly through teacher modeling. From these activities, two important concepts emerged: we began to show students that reading is a process, not magic, and we engaged in a more meaningful discussion of strategies that good readers use. We wanted the strategies to come from the students rather than handing them a chart in the beginning of the year, as we had done previously. We wanted them to see that all readers use strategies. *You already do these things*, we told them. *We are just going to help you become aware of them and gain more control over using them.*

Although this new approach gave students more ownership of strategies and helped them begin to see their own processes, creating the chart was still our goal. We still wanted to put the strategies into our students' hands, giving them a neat package of "good reader" tools rather than delving into the complexity of the reading process. After a few weeks, we again gave students the chart, asking them to memorize the strategies and assuming that they would apply them to their reading. We returned to business as usual: teaching strategies for the purpose of checking them off the list rather than assessing in ways that would show us if students were able to use these strategies to comprehend challenging subject-area texts.

Although students again showed progress in this second year in terms of reading more and gaining more confidence and interest in reading, it was clear at the end of the year that the big picture of understanding reading as a problem-solving process was still a bit fuzzy to both teachers and students. Students knew that there were strategies they could use to comprehend difficult text but were still unable to decipher how and when strategies helped them comprehend; they had not yet learned to use strategies flexibly, with a clear sense of purpose. Teachers knew that students were missing this valuable piece but continued to rely on practice with primarily narrative texts at or close to students' independent reading levels.

Year Three of Academic Literacy

As we began to plan for the third year of our program, two things were essential. First, we needed to continue to build on the strategies students already used while focusing a great deal more on the context for these strategies: reading as a process. Second, we needed to keep our long-term goal in mind when creating the beginning units: students must be prepared to tackle challenging academic texts in the second semester.

We began by reorganizing the curriculum, shifting the focus of our units from individual strategies that we wanted students to *practice* to essential questions that captured what we wanted students to *understand*. These essential questions emphasize what we want students to know by the end of each unit and give both teachers and students a context for using strategies. For example, the essential question for our second unit is, "What is reading?" Rather than explain to students that reading is a complex process that involves more than decoding words, we ask students the essential question and make sure that we design lesson plans that help them gain insight into an answer. By shifting our focus away from the chart of strategies to the more complex issues revealed in the essential questions, our lessons on individual strategies had a clearer purpose to us and to our students.

We realized that we needed to acknowledge more clearly that students come with their own stories, skills, biases, strategies, hang-ups, and interests, and we needed to build on them. If any significant changes were to be made in students' lives (both academic and personal), we needed to create a curriculum that allowed us to get to know students as readers and, more important, to help students know themselves in the context of reading. We needed to stop ignoring the cries that they "hated" reading and ask them why. We needed to use the data we had been gathering about our students to individualize instruction and guide the curriculum. We needed to put aside our frustration with a lack of one-on-one time and create that time.

We also needed to dazzle and engage students. Since 85 to 90 percent of our freshmen take Academic Literacy (the forty honors freshmen are allowed to take an elective), we have quite a range of abilities in one classroom. Many students had come from reading classes in middle school that focused on remediation. The groans of the first day revealed that few, if any, had faith that this class would be valuable. We had to convince them that Academic Literacy would help them become expert readers. Some of the groans came from highly skilled students who would have been in honors had they been identified as gifted in middle school or demonstrated earlier in the year the desire and skills to tackle a challenging curriculum. They often felt this class was beneath them.

We believed that Academic Literacy could be tailored to meet students individual pace and needs and benefit both struggling and advanced readers by pushing them out of their comfort zone, demanding that they tackle various genres, including standardized tests as a type of reading. We realized that if we wanted to create an environment in which all students believed that they were doing something valuable, they needed to see from the first day of school that Academic Literacy builds on their individual strengths and helps them address their weaknesses. Students also needed to feel that the classroom was a safe and welcoming place. Thus, we created the first unit of the year: Who Am I as a Reader?

The Academic Literacy Course: Who Am I as a Reader?

This first unit echoes themes from Unit 1, Reading Self and Society, in the Academic Literacy class described in *Reading for Understanding*. Many of the readings found in *An Anthology for Reading Apprenticeship* can be used for this unit, although we mention only a few. Exhibit 3.1 maps out the five weeks of the unit, and Exhibit 3.2 provides the curriculum for a sample week.

**Exhibit 3.1. Curriculum Overview of Unit 1:
Who Am I as a Reader?**

Essential questions	Who am I as a reader today?
	Why is reading important to me?
	What are my literacy goals for this year and beyond?
	How will Academic Literacy help me reach my goals?
Unit objectives	Awaken the reader within each student
	Familiarize students with routines and expectations for Academic Literacy
	Assess students' abilities and reading backgrounds in order to individualize the curriculum
	Help students create learning goals that reflect their awareness of their strengths and weaknesses and show them that Academic Literacy can help them attain these goals
Ongoing daily routines	Warm-up (5 minutes)
	Mini-lesson (10–15 minutes)
	Sustained silent reading (20–30 minutes)
	Share-out (5–10 minutes)
Readings	*How I Discovered Words*, by Malcolm X
	Reading for Success, by Richard Rodriguez
	Convicted in the Womb, by Carl Upchurch
	The Voice You Hear When You Read Silently, by Thomas Lux
	A Place to Stand, by Jimmy Santiago Bacca
	I Wanna Be Average, by Mike Rose
	Individually chosen books for silent sustained reading
Assessments	Complete a reading survey
	Degrees of Reading power (DRP) test
	California Achievement Test (CAT)
	Set up reading portfolios

Exhibit 3.1. *continued*

Goal setting	Reflection on reading survey
	Self-evaluation of DRP and CAT results
	Set goals for Academic Literacy: pick at least one goal for the rest of the quarter
	Place yourself on the "Why People Read" chart (based on writing a letter or essay, interview with the teacher, and/or whole class discussion)
Reading, writing, and reflection routines	Introduce and practice metacognitive logs, homework logs, talking to the text
	Introduce class routines and begin silent reading
	Write about reading history (essay, letter, story map)
	Warm-up or poster: Your favorite book
	Warm-up and discussion: How you use literacy now
	Warm-up and discussion: Future goals and how literacy figured into them
	Genre discussion: What kinds of reading materials are out there? What do you like?
Related activities	Do a reading process write based on the topic "How I Discovered Words"
	Create a "Why People Read" chart based on readings
	Develop a "Good Readers" poster
	Discuss how to choose a book
Additional suggested activities	Create "Banners and Stars" to post in the classroom for books students finish
	Write a review or create a book jacket for favorite book
	Do a "book tasting" of all the books in the classroom
	Complete a paired interview on reading habits
	Conduct a reading poll, interviewing people about what they read for work, in their daily lives, for pleasure

Exhibit 3.2. Week 5 Curriculum for Unit 1: Who Am I as a Reader?

	Monday	Tuesday	Wednesday	Thursday	Friday
Warm-up	• Read a model (written by the teacher) of reading letter (Who am I as a reader? Why do I read?); write down two questions	• Write about one of the events on your personal reading history map • "Give One, Get One": share an event from your life map with at least three other students	• Use your time line, "Good Reader" poster, CAT and DRP results, and other assessment data as resources for brainstorming some goals you have for this quarter	• Read the class list of goals for the quarter and choose two; write about your choices	• Reread your letter about who you are as a reader and why you read
Mini-lesson	• Reading letters: talk about what they are and how they work	• Discuss "stop-point" reflections in reading logs in response to sentence starters during SSR	• Create a class list of Academic Literacy goals	• Talk about how to link reading goals in your life now to your goals in the future	• Discuss what to include in your reading letter

	Monday	Tuesday	Wednesday	Thursday	Friday
Reading/writing	• Write a letter to the teacher about what you're reading	• SSR: stop at one point for reflection in your log	• SSR: stop at two points for reflection in your log	• SSR: After reading, reflect in your log—How can the reading logs help you achieve your literacy goals?	• Write a letter addressing who you are as a reader and why you read
Sharing out	• Share what you're reading for SSR	• Share one event from your personal reading history map	• Share out stop-point reflections from logs	• Share one goal	• Share one idea from your reading letter
Homework	• Complete your personal reading history map for tomorrow (begun in class in Week 4)				

Objectives

The following objectives for "Who Am I as a Reader?" build the foundation for our work throughout the year:

- Awakening the reader within each student

- Establishing routines and expectations for the class

- Assessing students' abilities and reading backgrounds in order to individualize the curriculum

- Helping students create learning goals that reflect their awareness of their strengths and weaknesses and show them that Academic Literacy can help them attain these goals

Awakening the Reader Within

From the moment students walk into our rooms on the first day of the new school year, we are trying to figure out who they are as readers, as students, as adolescents. We know that their experiences in reading and life have shaped their identity as readers—both positively and negatively. It is our job to build on their positive experiences and, often more challenging, to break down their negative attitudes. Students enter our classrooms with a variety of damaging beliefs about reading: reading is "boring"; reading requires a talent that some people are born with and others missed out on; reading is important only for people in a select group of professions, which does not include sports stars, nurses, or lawyers! Many students have fond memories of reading in their early years of elementary school, but the loss of choice and the shift to reading to learn made them lose interest. Most of the first unit of Academic Literacy focuses on helping students see that their "hate" of reading is a lack of interest and frustration with the difficulties of reading.

Sharing Stories About Reading

Teachers often think of modeling in terms of demonstrating skills or procedures. To us, modeling also means modeling vulnerability, honesty, and sharing. If we are asking students to explore who they are as readers and share their stories in a public forum with twenty others, we need to be willing to do the same. In Academic Literacy, teachers share not only their expertise as readers but some of their experiences with reading as well. One teacher might simply share her own reading survey (Appendix E provides a sample reading survey given at the beginning and end of the course), while another might give a book talk on the books that have influenced him or her the most.

One of us (Lisa) has a story she shares with students that she has found to be unique among English teachers and, especially, among reading teachers: "I was essentially a nonreader until college. While I received excellent grades in high school, I read only two books in their entirety: *To Kill a Mockingbird* by Harper Lee and *Anthem* by Ayn Rand. I share this with my students, and after they have moaned enough about how much they wish they could do the same, I read them an essay I wrote in college. The following is an excerpt from that paper, which deals with both my long-time love of writing and my newfound joy in reading":

> I envied my friends who were the bookworms. At least they had a name. What do you call a girl who carries around a beat-up old notebook as if it contained the meaning of life? The funny thing is, it did. My meaning of life consisted of recording my thoughts, observations, and emotions, making them a concrete extension of myself, to be analyzed, appreciated, disregarded by my own worst critic—me. Unfortunately, I never read. Not until my freshman year in college did I read my own autobiography. Or so it seemed that *Harriet the Spy* by Louise Fitzhugh spoke to me in a language all my own,

sparking memories of my childhood and affirming my thoughts and desires. Enrolled in a children's literature course, I finally read many of the books I had neglected in my childhood years of football, skateboarding, and, of course, writing. Out of all the books my adult mind consumed that year, *Harriet the Spy* undoubtedly pierced the innermost layer of my onion, as Harriet would say. If I had read *Harriet the Spy* at age nine, however, I would have understood my passion for writing earlier in life. Harriet undoubtedly would have been my heroine.

In addition, says Lisa, "I also talk to my students about why I hated to read as an adolescent: I thought I was a slow—and subsequently terrible—reader. I often had trouble focusing from page to page. Their mouths drop as I tell them I thought reading was *boring*, and still, to this day, sometimes do if I don't have the right book in my hand. I try to both impress on them that I feel I missed out on something and inspire them to think about reading as a way of finding out about themselves, something very few adolescents find boring."

Not all teachers feel comfortable sharing personal stories, but it is important for students to see real-life situations in which reading has had an impact, positive or negative. Readings from *An Anthology for Reading Apprenticeship* are very helpful in this regard. Many students revere Malcolm X for his work during the civil rights movement but are unfamiliar with the transformation he describes in the excerpt "Learning to Read." Malcolm X says that he had "never been so truly free in [his] life" until, while in prison, he discovered the joy and power of reading. We invite students to discuss the word *free*, and the idea of being mentally free in the world of books, with an example that is tangible.

It is also important to note that much of the Academic Literacy curriculum involves getting students interested in something, *anything*, not just books. Each year, many students indicate in their reading autobiographies that they do not have any topics they are interested in reading about. *None.* They have no idea what to put on a list of topics, let alone genres or authors, that they might like to explore. And we are shocked when these students proclaim that reading is boring? Their minds are bored! In "Learning to Read," Malcolm X also says, "The ability to read awoke inside [me] some long dormant craving to be mentally alive." One of the most important jobs for the Academic Literacy teacher may be to challenge students to suspend their disbelief in the power of reading, find books that inspire them, and awaken that dormant craving to be mentally alive.

Sharing Favorite Books

In order to awaken these readers, we use a number of activities encouraging students to find books at their independent reading level that they can connect to. We ask students to bring in their favorite book from any phase of their lives—from picture books to last year's classics—and to share them with their peers. This simple activity leads students to many realizations: *I didn't always hate reading. Other people like the same books I do. Reading in this class will not always be about books I don't like; I may have some choice.*

This activity serves as a reservoir of ideas, emotions, and interests that students can return to for the rest of the year. Recommendations from peers who seem to lack interest in reading are much more influential than the teacher's recommendations. Overlap in choice, such as frequent mention of S. E. Hinton's *The Outsiders* and Maurice Sendak's *Where the Wild Things Are,* helps create a sense of community and nostalgia for reading from a time before many students were soured by academic reading. Also, since this activity is nonthreatening, students feel free to bring in children's books such as those by Dr. Seuss; everybody is included.

Choosing Books

A plethora of activities are born from this student-generated pile of books. Conversations about how to find great books naturally stem from this activity. We have students create a poster, "How to Pick a Good Book," in which they list the aspects they consider when choosing books of interest. Although it is premature to delve deeply into concepts such as genre, this is a time to talk about the types of books students are naturally attracted to: sports, romance, and the ever-popular horror. Identifying students' interests both validates them and allows us a window into who they are as readers.

When introducing her mini-lesson on how to choose books, Beth starts by asking her students to explain the criteria they use for deciding what movie to rent at the video store. Students excitedly talk about friends' recommendations, the types of movies they love, such as comedies or horror movies, and their favorite actors. Some students talk about reading the back of the video case or looking at the picture on the front of it. The connections here to book recommendations, genre, and author are obvious to us but, surprisingly, not to them.

Creating Personal Reading History Maps

We ask students to reflect on their attitudes about reading and find ways to change negative attitudes or practice positive behaviors. For example, we ask them to create a personal reading history map, a visual representation or time line that traces their earliest to most recent memories about reading. This activity is often very informative for both the teacher and the student because it eliminates the roadblock of writing that many students face in conveying their ideas. Students can draw the map and simply label important events with few, if any, words. While many students simply go through the motions, listing facts such as grade levels and teachers' names, others reveal memories that spark great discussion and create a personal connection between the student and reading and the teacher and student. Students remember sitting on the floor in kindergarten as the teacher read Mother Goose tales; feeling like a failure when they were held back in second grade because they could not read; reading the one book that they believed contained the meaning of life.

Although it can be risky in a classroom setting, we find that the surfacing of these early memories is an essential step in the process of changing students' long-held beliefs about reading. Of course, teachers must create a safe environment in the classroom, where students feel free to share their stories about reading without fear of censure or humiliation, or students might shut down and add this as another negative reading memory.

Library Visits

During the second week of class, we bring all of our students to the library. Our dedicated librarian, who has spent years familiarizing himself with young adult literature, does a series of book talks on his favorites and gives students advice about how to find books in the library that they might enjoy.

During this first library visit, we spend the entire period looking for books rather than stressing the technical side of using the library. We ask students to choose at least three books to "taste" before returning to the classroom, one of which must be based on a recommendation from a teacher, a peer, or the librarian. We also encourage them to use the ideas from the "How to Pick a Good Book" poster and to use the "five finger rule" in order to locate a book that is not too difficult for them. According to the five finger rule, if a book has more than five words on a page the reader does not know, the book is too hard.

Establishing Routines and Expectations

Another important goal at the beginning of the year is establishing the routines and procedures for Academic Literacy. Our curriculum requires students to be on-task and self-directed, as well as willing to share personal experiences during class time. Students must know that our classrooms offer a safe and predictable environment, supported by regular routines and clear expectations.

Each day we strive to divide up class time in the following manner:

- Warm-up: five minutes

- Mini-lesson: ten to fifteen minutes

- Silent sustained reading: twenty to thirty minutes

- Share-out: five to ten minutes

Warm-Up

Teenagers have a million and one things on their minds that are more important to them than school. Thus, it is important that the first thing they do each day in Academic Literacy helps them focus and gets them into the reading mode. We have tried to begin class without a warm-up, and each time we have found ourselves having to give a lecture on appropriate behavior. Students need a quick focusing activity that helps them get settled and ready for the lesson of the day. During the warm-up, we require that students work independently and quietly. This is time for them to get down their ideas; sharing occurs in the mini-lesson or during the share-out time.

Depending on the lesson that day, we may ask students to do a number of different things as warm-ups. Typically, they will either do a quick write on a topic we select or read a short text they must respond to. We may ask students to write about the kinds of things that distract them while they read or describe their earliest reading memory. Quick writes, in which students are asked to write on a topic for five to ten minutes in a stream-of-consciousness manner, connect the content of the class to the things students have on their minds.

During the second week of class, we do a lesson on metacognition and the mental processes we go through while we read. For the warm-up, we ask students to read the Malcolm X piece "Learning to Read" and write about what was difficult about the piece and how they made sense of it. We like to use this piece early in the year as a hook because many of our students are familiar with Malcolm X and revere him; he is credible. We encourage students to notice the unconscious moves they make while they read, as well as the more obvious strategies they use to make sense of the piece. We purposely use a very open question—"Tell us what you are thinking and doing as you read"—to encourage an authentic response. The warm-up in this case focuses students on the topic of the day—reading as a process—and helps get them into the mode of reading strategically.

The Mini-Lesson

The ten- to fifteen-minute targeted mini-lesson involves teacher-directed, whole class instruction. The goal is to introduce concepts and strategies in an efficient manner in order to maximize the amount of student-centered time in the classroom. Although there are times when we have to be the "sage on the stage," we try to ensure that students have the bulk of the time to practice, share, and reflect on the information we are giving them.

Mini-lessons can range from the practical, such as routines of the class (how to check out books, how to organize the reading portfolio), to more abstract concepts related to metacognition and reading theory. The bulk of this time is spent on the reading strategies, either pulling them from student work or presenting them through modeling and direct instruction.

In mini-lessons, we may introduce a new strategy, modeling it with a think-aloud, illustrate effective reading log entries by reading student models, or invite discussions about students' beliefs and experiences with reading. For example, following the warm-up on Malcolm X's "Learning to Read," our mini-lesson involves students in creating two posters—one about what makes a text difficult to read and the other about different strategies students use to make sense of a text. In this mini-lesson, as in many others, we are not delivering a lecture on strategies; rather, we are eliciting examples from students' shared experience with reading a difficult text. As we ask students to share what was difficult about reading the text and what they did to make sense of it, we help them with language to describe their experiences and solutions, but all the ideas come from them. This lesson, illustrated by the sample responses in Exhibit 3.3, allows students to see the wealth of strategies they as readers can and do employ.

Another example of a mini-lesson that should be done early in the year is generating a "Good Readers" poster as a class. As a warm-up before this mini-lesson, students quietly brainstorm things

Exhibit 3.3. Student Responses to a Mini-Lesson on Making Sense of Text

What Makes a Text Difficult to Read
- Lack of prior knowledge
- Difficult vocabulary
- Long, complicated sentences
- Use of metaphors makes it difficult to get meaning
- Unknown references to people, places, or events in history

What Students Do to Make Sense of Text
- Define unknown words
- Reread sentences or paragraphs they don't understand
- Visualize the people, places, and situations
- Read in a quiet place
- Write down key words
- Define words in context (use context clues)
- Use clues to guess the meaning of the paragraph
- Imagine themselves in the place of the character
- Read on to see if confusion clears up
- Skim to look for the main ideas
- Make connections to their own knowledge and lives
- Use prior knowledge to make sense of the text
- Take notes
- Slow down to understand the book
- Consider the beat of the language
- Block out distractions and concentrate

they think good readers do. We encourage students to write down anything that comes to mind. Exhibit 3.4 is an example of poster from the beginning of the year.

This activity generates a great deal of debate, surfacing many misconceptions students have about reading. Inevitably, some students will say things such as, "Good readers understand everything they read" or "Good readers read the fastest." Teachers can dispel many of the myths and seize this opportunity to explore how complex reading is and how all readers struggle with text, but good readers use tools to overcome difficulties.

Last year, one group of students steadfastly argued at the beginning of the year that "good readers are always good spellers." Because these initial weeks focus on excavating student knowledge and beliefs, the teacher created a new poster for things the class would investigate throughout the year. The question, "Are good readers always good spellers?" stayed on the poster, along with other questions that came up during the year, until May, when students realized that their teacher—in their eyes, a great reader—was not, in fact, the best speller.

Exhibit 3.4. Student Responses to a Mini-Lesson on What Good Readers Do

Good Readers:
- Get help when they are confused
- Adjust their reading rate depending on text difficulty
- Read a lot
- Ask questions
- Make predictions
- Relate to the reading
- Survey the text before reading
- Try to picture what they're reading
- Guess unknown vocabulary words
- Look up unknown vocabulary words
- Think about what they are reading

Silent Sustained Reading

In our Academic Literacy class routine, mini-lessons are followed by silent sustained reading (SSR), which often is the longest segment of the class. Ideally, students will put the concept or skill covered in the mini-lesson into practice during SSR. In SSR, students usually read self-selected high-interest books at or close to their independent reading level. However, we periodically require the class to read the same text, particularly at the beginning of the year, when we need to direct the discussion. The selections in the *An Anthology for Reading Apprenticeship* are useful for introducing strategies while discussing an important topic in the first unit: the power of literacy.

It is imperative that we give students time to read in class. For most of our students, SSR is the only time in the entire day when they read. Equally important is that students are held accountable for engaging with the text. The task must be structured, and teachers must monitor student behavior. This is difficult even in a class of only twenty students. Many SSR programs fail students by allowing them to circumvent the system. An observation in another teacher's classroom revealed a student who appeared to be faithfully reading during SSR. Because there were few activities in this class that held students accountable for the reading, he received a good grade in the reading class. However, he was failing the second hour of the block: English. When we asked him why there seemed to be a discrepancy between his performance in Academic Literacy and the traditional English class, we expected to hear an insightful comment about lack of choice in reading materials or books that were just "boring." To our surprise, he proudly confided a secret: "I learned this trick. I learned how to sleep with my eyes open."

Metacognitive Logs

Metacognitive logs are a tool we use to ensure that students are accountable for engaging with the text and not sleeping with their eyes open. At the beginning of the year, before we have time to go into depth about strategies or metacognition, the logs help students begin practicing the crucial mental processes that proficient readers use. Many of our initial mini-lessons deal with how to use the logs, why they are set up the way they are, and how they connect with the curriculum for the year.

The logs are divided into three sections:

• Prereading. In the prereading section of the log, students are typically asked to activate their prior knowledge and make predictions about what will happen in that day's reading. We require students to give evidence for their predictions. This forces students to think about what they have read and connect it to what they will read next. It also ensures that students make thoughtful predictions.

• During reading. In this section of the log, students are asked to stop at two different places in the text and complete sentence stems such as "I got confused when . . ." or "I finally understand that . . . ." These stopping points force students to read actively and check their comprehension. One of the greatest challenges is getting students to stop and reflect rather than plow through the reading. Although some complain that stopping interrupts their reading, these sentence stems help them practice what strategic readers do. They also provide evidence that students are engaging with the text and offer valuable insight into students' levels of comprehension.

• After reading. The after-reading section of the log changes the most throughout the year. As the year progresses, we modify the logs to reflect the particular strategy or concept we are working on in each unit. For example, in the first unit, we use three different logs. Although all of the logs ask students to predict before they read and to select from a list of stems to write about during reading, the prompt changes depending on the focus for that week. Because students have a great deal of difficulty focusing during SSR at the beginning of the year, the first after-reading prompt asks them to note the distractions they encountered while reading and create action plans to overcome these distractions. Depending on how quickly a particular class can focus during SSR, the second after-reading prompt is introduced, which asks students to analyze their reading process. This log parallels our initial reading process writes, in which students are given a short piece of text to read and asked to articulate what they are doing to make sense of it, and our discussion of reading as a process. The third after-reading prompt asks students to note the confusions they had while reading and what steps they took to clear up these confusions.

At each interval, students are asked to think about their reading and either apply a strategy or reflect on their reading process in writing.

In later units, when we go into depth about particular strategies, the logs reflect each focus. For example, during the unit focused on questioning, the prereading prompt asks students to write down a question that they want answered by the end of the reading. The during-reading sentence starters for this log all relate to various methods of questioning, such as "on the surface and under the surface" questions or the four types of questions in question-answer relationships.[2] The after-reading prompt asks students to answer their questions and create one more that they can keep in mind while doing their reading homework that night. Other after-reading prompts might ask students to summarize what they read that day, clarify one problem that they had, or talk about how schema affected their reading of a particular book.

During the first part of the year, we guide students through the sections of the reading log in a structured fashion. Before we begin reading for the day, we ask everyone to respond to the prereading prompt, which asks them to predict what they think will happen in their reading for the day. We then ask a few students to share their predictions, and we focus on the evidence they used to support this prediction. After students have read silently for about five to ten minutes, we ask them to find a comfortable place to stop their reading and respond to one of the during-reading sentence starters. We repeat this procedure after another five to ten minutes. Then we ask a few students to share their responses at this stopping point with the class. Finally, at the end of the silent reading time, we ask students to respond to the after-reading prompt and again encourage several students to share their ideas.

Throughout this process, we encourage students to be more specific in their comments, gently pointing out why comments such as "I got confused when I didn't understand what was happening" are not specific enough to help them improve their comprehension. (How many times a day do we ask students to tell us what they do not understand, only to have them shrug their shoulders and say "I don't know" or, after ten minutes of directions, "All of it"?) The heart of metacognition is getting students to identify *what* they do not understand so they can tackle the problem strategically. Insightful comments on the logs such as this one reveal that students are doing just that: "I got confused when all of a sudden Helen was telling a story about how her mom could really cook and then she popped out with a dream [in which] she saw Laurie with evil eyes and it was the mirror girl."

As is often the case, since teachers cannot read every teen pulp novel our students choose, we have no idea who the "mirror girl" is or why Helen was talking about her mother's cooking. What is clear, however, is that this student noticed that a break in her comprehension occurred and figured out that the dream sequence was the cause of her confusion.

Because there is not enough time to discuss every response to the logs, we choose representative comments to share from which the class can learn something about their reading. The comment stimulates discussion about how the student figured out it was a dream. When did she realize it wasn't real? Did she reread? Did she have to keep reading and set aside her confusion in order to get more information? This last strategy is especially valuable to emphasize, because many students give up or forget that the answer to questions that are raised in the reading may appear after the confusing part. They do not realize that they may not have missed something; the author may *want* them to be confused. At this point, we can add a question to the poster "What makes text difficult to read?" Dream sequences and narrative shifts are common problems in both books and, as students like to discuss, movies.

This routine for using reading logs may seem forced, and it is. However, as we explain to students, this structure is the best way we know to get them to begin to see and internalize the unconscious moves that proficient readers make. After one or two weeks of this targeted work with logs, most students are comfortable with the routine, and we do not need to stop them at each interval. Once the routine is established, we stress that they should try to use the stop-point time to write down their natural thoughts about the book. We encourage them to listen to their "reader voices" during silent reading and use the logs simply to track their thinking.

Share-Out

The final portion of the class is a whole class share-out. This is often the shortest portion of the class (five to ten minutes), but in many ways the most important because we ask students to link the lesson of the day to their experiences with reading. For example, if the focus that day is on noticing distractions, we ask students to talk about the kinds of things that distracted them during SSR and how they refocused themselves. We also make sure to extend the conversation to how this process of refocusing might look when they read in their other classes or for homework at night. Other typical share-out topics focus on their progress with their SSR books, their responses to log prompts, or book recommendations.

Share-out should be the time to engage students, especially shy, quiet students who often become invisible in class, in talking about their books in a brief, informal, nonthreatening forum. Share-outs can be done in whole class discussion or in pairs to maximize student involvement. The most important thing to remember is that whole class discussion does not mean everyone else sleeps or chats while the teacher and one student converse. If share-out time is to be meaningful rather than detrimental to the class, students must feel that this important work they are doing with books and their new-found excitement are not falling on deaf ears. We look for ways to probe and to make the personal relevant to the entire class: *Is anyone else reading a romance novel? Are you finding some of the same elements? What could this reader do to deal with the confusions he is sharing? This character is experiencing a typical conflict in a coming-of-age novel; has anyone else in here ever felt like that? Why would a teenager feel that way?* These kinds of questions add depth to the reader's understanding of the novel and allow others to engage in the exploration of that character. The share-out is the best time to encourage students to be thoughtful not only about their reading in Academic Literacy but about links to their other classes and to their worlds.

Assessing Students' Reading Abilities and Reading Background

Another objective for the first unit is to assess students' interests and abilities using a variety of methods, such as standardized tests, anecdotal data, teacher observation, and student self-reflection. Students are often given reading assessments for the purpose of sorting and placing them in classes or programs. As a result, students have come to see assessment as something that is done *to* them rather than as part of a process they can learn from. Using a variety of assessments, both qualitative and quantitative, at the beginning of Academic Literacy gives teachers a more nuanced view of students' reading and gives students access to information that can help them better understand themselves as readers.

Quantitative Assessments

Two standardized tests help us determine the reading level of our students. The California Achievement Test (CAT), which consists of a vocabulary section and a reading comprehension section closely resembling standardized reading tests students take in California, gives us an approximate grade level for a student's reading. The

average reading level for our entering freshmen has remained consistent at approximately sixth-grade reading level over the past three
years. The range of their entering reading levels as measured by this
test is from second grade to twelfth grade. The other standardized
test we use, the Degrees of Reading Power (DRP) test, is a cloze
reading test that provides a national percentile ranking (see Appendix G). Because the CAT is somewhat outdated, we do not recommend purchasing it, but we like to use these two tests together since
they give students practice with and confidence in negotiating two
very different test formats.

There are numerous practice tests popping up in this new era of
emphasis on the standardized testing, and we recommend finding
one that yields the particular information you are looking for. Many
schools rely on students' Stanford Achievement Test (SAT 9) scores
as another measure of ability, and we consider these as well.

We have reservations about the testing culture thrust on us. But
we know that testing is a reality, and if testing is handled well, having access to test data allows both teachers and students a starting
point for setting goals and monitoring improvement. We believe
that standardized tests should be used as just one part of a broader
set of multiple measures. We also believe that talking to students
about standardized tests as a genre—about the various formats,
skills required, types of directions—is a key to helping students gain
some control over these gatekeeping mechanisms that will affect
their academic opportunities.

Qualitative Assessments

More important than these quantitative measures are a variety of
qualitative assessments that give both teachers and students win-
dows into students' learning and reading process:

• Reading surveys. Through a reading survey, we find out which
students like to read, which students have family members who read,
whether they think they are good readers and why, and who their

favorite authors are. We also find out about student beliefs about reading in general: Why do people read? Is reading important? What do good readers do while reading? We do not help or prompt students in any way because we want to get an accurate picture of their habits and beliefs. Students complete the same survey at the end of the year in order to see if these habits and beliefs have changed.

• Reading process writes. Reading process writes are a window into our students' skills. We have already discussed the importance of uncovering the strategies students already use, and reading process writes are an important tool to do this. In what we call a *reading process write*, we give students a short piece to read and ask them to articulate what they are doing to make sense of the text. It is extremely important that students are given a text that is challenging since a text that is too easy will not require students to work to comprehend it. It is also important that students are not prompted by the teacher since we are looking for what students actually do, not what they think we want to hear or what their previous reading teacher thought was important. Therefore, the first process write is less structured than the rest. We simply ask students to write an entire page about what they do to understand the text. Many students are baffled. They are, of course, using strategies when reading, as all readers do, but they lack insight into their process or the language with which to talk about it. It is just as important for students to express their confusion as it is for them to note strategies such as rereading and of connecting the material to their own experiences.

As the year progresses, the process writes become more specific. We typically ask students to write about three questions while reading a text:

• What makes this text difficult to read?

• What are you doing to try to comprehend this text?

• How did you feel reading this piece?

The first question asks students to break down difficult reading into obstacles that can be overcome. Students often realize that "long sentences" can make them stumble, even if the vocabulary is simple. Then teachers can help students make the connection to the second question—how to deal with these long sentences—and discuss various methods, such as chunking, finding the main clause, or breaking sentences down into parts of speech. In order to make this a truly meaningful assessment, teachers must push students beyond just naming strategies. We encourage students who simply list strategies to explain how they use them and how and when these strategies help them make sense of text. Specific examples are always helpful. Many students who have had reading classes in previous years try to dazzle us with the list of strategies they used to understand the piece. But on further inspection, we often find that students are naming strategies incorrectly or, worse, engaging in a much more complex process than can be conveyed in one word. This process has to be broken down for any real communication to occur between student and teacher, student and student, and student and self. At the end of the year, students and teachers can compare their early process writes to their final paper, the reflective reading letter, to gauge whether students are more metacognitive.

• Personal reading history maps, reading histories, and journals. Students who struggle with reading often struggle with writing as well. Creative projects, such as personal reading history maps in which students draw a map of their reading experiences beginning with their earliest memories, can provide insight into students' backgrounds through a less threatening medium than writing. Reading histories give students opportunities to delve more deeply through writing into incidents they may have included in their reading history maps. We invite students to write about experiences that have shaped them as readers. These may include early memories of reading or being read to and more recent incidents involving reading in school and in other areas of their lives. What emerges from these histories is a deeper understanding for both students and the teacher of how students' experiences have shaped their attitudes about reading and their image of themselves as readers. We also ask students to respond to their reading in journals. When asking students to write in response to journal prompts, we assure them that at this stage, content is more important than spelling, mechanics, or organization.

• Think-aloud conferences. Think-aloud conferences are a powerful tool for teachers to see how students are processing text. Done early in the year, they reveal a lot about students' reading processes, but only after students have had some training and practice with this method. In this type of conference, we meet with students one-on-one and ask them to do a think-aloud on an unfamiliar text, stopping occasionally to talk about what they are doing and thinking about as they read. We want to see whether students are being metacognitive about their reading. This is evident if they stop several times while they are reading and discuss the confusions they have, connections they make, and strategies they are using to make sense of the text. It is helpful for the teacher to record what students are doing naturally on a T-chart, with one column labeled "What the Student Says" and the other labeled "Comments/Questions/Analysis." These initial observations are valuable for planning activities and discussion with students about the reading process.

• Informal miscue analysis. In an initial conference, students bring a book they are reading for SSR. We ask them to open to a page they have not already read and read aloud. While they are reading, we do a very informal miscue analysis, making a hash mark for every word they read correctly and writing down the words that they struggle with or decode incorrectly.

Helping Students Create Learning Goals

Around the beginning of the third week, we ask students to reflect on the various assessments we have done. Our intentions here are twofold. First, we want students to be aware of their strengths and weaknesses so they may help direct their time in the class. We also want students to have a realistic picture of how they perform on standardized tests. These tests are one measure of their reading abilities, and we owe our students an honest discussion about this reality. Students who perform well are often surprised and delighted with their results. These students are nevertheless expected to reflect on their strengths and come up with goals for improvement. We are quick to warn them that this class will not be easy but that we will expect them to excel regardless of their test scores. Second, we want to assure students who have been told over and over again that they are poor readers that we believe—that we *expect*—they will improve as readers. Only about 15 percent of students in the ninth grade enter reading at grade level, so many of our students have been made to feel stupid. We gather quotations from students in previous Academic Literacy classes and share some of these success stories with our students. One student commented, "My teacher [in Academic Literacy] inspired me to read and that changed my attitude from eighth grade. I never thought that I could read fourteen books in one school year but I did. I was really surprised when I saw how much my book list was filling up and I thank my teacher for helping me do that."

All students can set high goals regardless of their skills because these goals are both quantitative, such as raising a score on an exam, and qualitative, such as changing behaviors and attitudes about reading. For example, students are asked to reflect on their standardized test scores and create realistic goals for the posttest at the end of the year. We want to challenge them to improve their skills, but we coach them to set realistic goals. If a student who scored a 33 out of 70 on the DRP test notes that her goal is to score a perfect 70 by the end of the year, we talk to her and together decide on an ambitious yet realistic goal. If a student scored a perfect 70 on the DRP (which rarely happens), we inform that student that she can take a more challenging level of the DRP at the end of the year. However, it is more important for this student to be praised for her achievement and expected to think of other ways she can challenge herself to excel in Academic Literacy.

We ask students to think more broadly about how Academic Literacy can help them as readers. As a class, we brainstorm a variety of goals from "reading more" to "reading a wide variety of genres" to "finishing books we start." We leave room at the bottom of the poster for additional ideas as they come up in our conversations about books and reading. We sometimes add our own teacher goals too. Exhibit 3.5 shows a poster with sample goals for readers that students brainstormed and a section of teacher goals.

Individualizing Instruction

We believe in grouping students heterogeneously in Academic Literacy. We have found that tracking students in higher and lower Academic Literacy classes, as we tried to do our first year, is often based on faulty and limited assessments, is detrimental to "remedial" readers, and is simply unnecessary. Even if all students were at the same reading level, there would still be great variability in their strengths, weaknesses, and motivations as readers. Because of the diversity in our students' academic preparation, much of the success of this initial unit and the class in general depends on our ability to tailor the curriculum to the needs of each student. This can seem like a daunting task when the teacher is faced with a classroom of twenty (or, in some schools, thirty-five) students. However, within the context of a well-run Academic Literacy class, it is possible. Three main activities allow us to meet the unique needs and interests of our students: conferencing, reading letters, and literature circles.

Conferencing

One of the most effective ways to individualize instruction is by meeting with students one-on-one. Although individual attention is a challenge in any classroom, the silent sustained reading time, if used wisely, is the perfect time for individual conferences.

During the first two to three weeks of class, we do not meet with any students individually because they need to become comfortable

Exhibit 3.5. Poster Displaying Sample Goals for Readers

Sample Goals for Readers
- Read every day.
- Read to your siblings, children, or parents.
- Learn to like or appreciate reading.
- Expand your vocabulary by reading challenging books, using new words in conversation, and using the dictionary.
- Finish books that you begin.
- Ignore distractions while reading.
- Read with other points of view in mind.
- Learn to read in your first language.
- Read a variety of genres.
- Practice decoding (sounding out) words.
- Try to understand where the plot is going by predicting or reading ahead.
- Improve reading aloud through practice.
- Find a good role model, and get tutoring.
- Read actively (by taking notes or asking questions) so you don't get bored.
- Get in the mood to read by predicting or activating your prior knowledge.
- Place yourself in the position of the character.
- Use preparation materials to improve SAT 9 scores.
- Expand your imagination by reading fantasy or science fiction books.

Teacher-Added Goals
- Read more books than you ever have before.
- Time yourself as a reader, and create goals for improving speed (but make sure you still understand what you read!).
- Read as fast as you can, trying to see chunks of words instead of one word at a time. Read for the meaning of the text, not to say the words.
- Experiment with skimming, skipping, and scanning.
- Read one book at a time so that you can focus.
- Develop consistent reading habits: set aside times and places you can expect to read.

Exhibit 3.5. *continued*

- Begin to identify the authors you love, and read more of their books.
- Ask for recommendations of good books from your friends and your teachers.
- Talk to other people about your books as much as possible.
- Remember to bring a book to class with you every day.
- Do not talk during silent reading so that you can concentrate!
- Write letters to your teacher or students in the class about your book.

Source: Many of the teacher's ideas are inspired by Atwell, N. *In the Middle: New Understandings About Writing and Learning.* (2nd ed.) Portsmouth, N.H.: Heinemann, 1998.

with the patterns of the class and practice both the "sustained" and "silent" aspects of SSR. These first few weeks are better spent modeling appropriate behavior by reading with students, monitoring their focus by silently circulating while students are reading, recording their page progress on a chart, and using body language (such as placing a hand on the desk or shoulder of a student whose mind is drifting) to manage behavior. After the first few weeks, most students know what the classroom should look like, sound like, and feel like during SSR. At this point, we are ready to begin conferencing.

Informal Conferencing with Students

Keeping tabs on twenty different students reading twenty different books may seem like an impossible task. This monitoring is imperative, however, since it is so easy for students to fall through the cracks and, as we mentioned earlier, to sleep with their eyes open during SSR. A conference can be used to have the student read to us and discuss a book choice. Frequent, even daily, informal individual conferences help students maintain their focus and help the teacher keep track of how students are doing.

One way to connect with students daily is to walk the rows at the beginning of SSR, using a chart to record students' page number progress and making notations of forgotten books or book changes. The chart is simply a grid with students' names down the left and the days of the week across the top, with the boxes large enough for us to write notations. This simple system has numerous benefits. First, the close physical proximity to students helps them settle down and focus during SSR time. Second, this is a great time to make a personal connection with each student. We cheer on students who are almost finished with their books, have brief interactions about books we are familiar with, express any concerns about the level of a book a student is reading, thank a student for coming to class prepared, or simply say good morning. Third, this easy record-keeping system shows us at a glance how students are moving through a book. If a student appears to be on page 70 of a book one day and page 34 of the same book the next or returns the next day claiming to have completed thirty minutes of reading homework, only to be on the same page as the day before, this is the time to inquire whether the student is rereading or faking reading. If a student seems to be averaging three or four pages per day during thirty-five minutes of silent reading, either the book is too difficult or the student is not using his time well. We have a large space on the SSR chart to record important information such as "forgot book," "changed book," or "absent/tardy." Tracking patterns of attendance or behavior makes it easy to hold students accountable for their reading.

Moving into their territory, getting into close physical proximity to students, is part of our "guerrilla warfare" approach to individualizing the curriculum and engaging students in reading. We ambush them any chance we get, such as during a shift in activity or as they walk into class, and bombard them with book choices. We seek out those quiet students who want to blend into the background, demanding to know about the great books they are reading. And every now and then, we drop a bomb: we tell students to abandon a book! If a student has read the first few pages (at least ten), has no history of constantly abandoning books, and is still not engaged, we urge him or her to move on. There are too many great books in the world to waste time during independent reading with a book that is not engaging. We have turned around reluctant readers by simply taking notice of their interest, buying them a book, and handing it to them: *I saw this book, and I thought of you.*

By constantly talking to students individually about books rather than relying only on formal share-out time in the whole class, we show students our enthusiasm and interest. We invite students to explore who they are as readers in a very natural, comfortable way that they never would have shared in a formal setting.

Formal Conferences

Formal conferences, in which we expect to meet with every student in the class on a particular subject or to obtain specific information, occur ideally four times a year. At the beginning of the year, conferences typically focus on book choice, book difficulty level, and goal setting. Throughout the year, we meet with students to discuss logs and progress in the class and to set new goals. For example, after the class has generated the poster "Sample Goals for Readers," we ask students to pick two or three goals they would like to work on. We then take several days to meet with students one-on-one during silent reading time to read over their goals, discuss why they chose them, and hear what they plan on doing to achieve them. We make sure we acknowledge these goals officially in some way—writing "approved" on their goals if possible and setting up a follow-up date when we will have a conference about their progress.

A goal for number of pages read in the first quarter is the most tangible and telling for students. We ask students to calculate an average number of pages they are reading each day based on their logs and then project how many pages they could read during class each day and for homework. We allow students to adjust the number if a new book is particularly difficult or easy. Most students are shocked to see that even if they read only eight pages at each sitting, they could read almost a thousand pages in a quarter. This is very eye-opening for them and shows them that we have high expectations for their final counts.

Beth has this to say about her first conferences with students:

> The first time I meet with students in the beginning of the year, I try to spend about ten minutes with each student. This means I can get about two interviews done per silent reading session. While I walk the class on the day of conferences, I let the two students know that I will be meeting with them that day. I ask them to bring their books, reading portfolios, and an open mind.
>
> During these initial conferences I conduct mini-interviews in which I ask students what books they are reading, why they chose them, and if they plan on sticking with them. I also ask them to open to a page they have not read before and read it out loud to me. I believe this is the most important part of this first conference. I ask them to summarize what happened in that portion of the book and predict how it connects to the portion they have already read.
>
> I am looking for a few different things when I conduct this first interview. I want to see if they are picking books that are both interesting to them and at or near their independent reading level. In addition, I want to get a sense of their ability to summarize and predict. While they are reading, I do a very informal miscue analysis on a sticky note: I make a hash mark for every word they read correctly and write down the words that they struggle with or decode incorrectly. If a student shows 95 percent accuracy, I encourage her to finish the book. If a student exhibits less accuracy, I will explain to her that this book might not help her build fluency. If she is emotionally invested in the book, however, I may agree that

she can read it as a "challenge book" or encourage her to set it aside until she has more tools to comprehend it. I typically end this interview by talking to students honestly about what I see as their reading strengths and weaknesses and by adding one or two goals to their goal list.

Think-Aloud Conferences

We believe that think-aloud conferences are a powerful assessment tool early in the year to get a picture of whether students know how to be metacognitive and throughout the year to check on their progress in incorporating new strategies. For example, if we are teaching a strategy like clarifying, we might do a series of think-alouds to see how and when students make clarifications with text. It is important that students understand that in these conferences, we are not evaluating them on how well they comprehend the text but rather on how aware they are of when their comprehension breaks down and how they are developing strategies to "fix up" their understanding.

In the beginning of the year, we use a simple T-chart to record what students are doing. But as the year progresses and students learn about more strategies they can use, we can be more specific about what we are looking for. As students read and think aloud, we check off the various strategies they use and write comments for the debriefing on a chart such as the one shown in Exhibit 3.6. Our comments might be "student doesn't self-correct (just keeps on reading after saying words that do not make sense)," "student confirms predictions while reading," "asks questions but they seem to reveal little understanding of content," or "makes connections that seem to help her visualize the text."

Obviously, this kind of think-aloud is useful for both practice and assessment. When we meet with students in think-aloud conferences, we are able to see how they are, or are not, reading strategically and can give them pointers. For example, if a student does a think-aloud in which he simply reads through the text, we encourage him to stop

Exhibit 3.6. Think-Aloud Evaluation Form

Name: _____   Date: _____

Title of Text: _____

Strategy	Comments
1. Activating prior knowledge (thinking about what you already know before reading)	
2. Predicting (guessing what will happen later based on what you already know)	
3. Questioning (asking yourself questions as you read)	
4. Clarifying (making sure you understand something)	
5. Summarizing (stating the main idea in your own words)	
6. Identifying problems (I got confused when . . ., I'm not sure of . . ., I didn't expect . . .)	
7. Using fix-up strategies (I think I'll read ahead . . ., Let me think back . . ., Maybe I'll reread this . . .)	
8. Making connections (This is like . . ., This reminds me of . . .)	
9. Other	

every second paragraph and then prompt him to ask a question or make a comment.

Reviews of Progress

Two of the teachers in Academic Literacy meet formally with students several times throughout the year to review their progress in the class. They sit with students for ten to fifteen minutes and go through their reading portfolios, discussing progress on key assignments, logs, and silent reading. One teacher comes to these meetings prepared with sticky notes and shows students where they can deepen their thinking in their logs and in assignments such as their reading history. She also uses conference time to talk about their grade so far and how they can improve it.

Reading Letters

Reading letters are a written exchange between a student and teacher about books and reading. Teachers work with reading letters in different ways. One teacher has students write to her once a week (typically on Fridays) in a spiral-bound notebook. She responds to these letters and returns them the following week. Typically, she requires that students write a full page, addressing the way they are making sense of what they are reading, as well as their reactions to what they are reading.

Reading letters establish a dialogue between the teacher and students about their independent reading and their work with strategies. These letters are a powerful tool because they give the teacher a chance to "talk" one-on-one with students in a nonthreatening way. Furthermore, through our responses to students, we can model ways to think about books, formal and informal language used to talk about books, and various strategies we use when reading.

It is time-consuming for teachers to respond to reading letters, especially if teachers have more than one reading class. However, they truly seem to change the whole tenor of a class. Students respond very positively to this type of honest inquiry into their reading lives.

Inevitably, after three or four weeks of written dialogue through this letter exchange, students begin to open up honestly about their reading motivations, habits, and abilities.

Literature Circles

At the beginning of the year, students read books selected individually in order to generate excitement about reading, discover what they are interested in, and begin to determine their independent reading levels. However, it is also important that students engage in high-quality talk about text with both teachers and other students. Once some trust has been built between teacher and student, and student and books, we ask students to form a literature circle (sometimes called a book club) and read the same book as two or three other students in the class.[3] They meet periodically to engage in meaningful dialogue about books during which they, among other things, summarize what they have read, discuss connections, make predictions, clarify confusions, and ask questions.

Literature circles help individualize the curriculum for students in the areas of both interest and ability. Depending on the focus and curriculum guidelines for the course, students should have some choice of genre, topic, collaborative partnerships, and, most important, degree of difficulty of the book they read. Literature circles are the most successful activity we have found for engaging students who are struggling readers, as well as those who are planning to enroll in the honors or AP track the following year.

Although there are some benefits to grouping students heterogeneously, such as higher-level students serving as role models for students working at lower levels, we prefer to group students homogeneously in literature circles. This grouping allows us to push students to choose books that are challenging but accessible to them, no matter at what level they enter—or exit—the class. We require that honors candidates tackle a text from the honors curriculum and expect that they will engage in challenging conversation and deep analysis of the text. Literature circles give less experienced readers the opportunity to read a book a bit beyond their independent reading level and to draw on the social support of their peers to comprehend it.

While the groups meet, the teacher can circulate and help each group with targeted instruction at their level. We often use this time to teach the strategies and techniques that we feel a particular group can benefit from the most. Their work in the group as well as their performance on ongoing assessments guides our instruction for each group. For example, a higher-end group reading Mary Shelley's *Frankenstein* may need extended work on how to annotate their text using sticky notes, whereas a lower-end group reading David Pelzer's *A Child Called "It"* may benefit from some deeper instruction in and practice with summarizing.

Challenges and Next Steps

Individualizing our curriculum to meet the needs of each student has been the most difficult instructional challenge in Academic Literacy. Each of us has struggled with how to make the time to meet with and write to students about their reading and how to adjust the curriculum to meet the varying needs of all students. It is an enormous task and not one at which we always feel successful. For example, last year, Beth made it through initial conferences with students but was unable to meet with them for extended periods of time after that: "As curriculum pressures and management issues grew in my fifth period class I found myself less and less able to meet one on one for extended periods of time with students. I began to rely more on the brief talks I had with students while I recorded their reading progress and during the share-out portion of the class. Having said this, I still believe that this one-on-one time is the most important aspect of the Academic Literacy class." Our next goal is to focus more on this aspect of the class. It is our hope that every Academic Literacy teacher at Jefferson High School will pick three focal students to follow throughout the year. We will use the work and progress of these students as a focus for our discussions of ways to better individualize the curriculum.

Most students feel they have learned something by the time they complete Academic Literacy. The course has credibility in their eyes because of the complexity of the material. It requires new terminology, "lists" of information, and a sprinkling of reading theory. But have we created a new content that students are expected to master rather than developing a class that helps them make sense of the content of the high school curriculum?

As we have revised our Academic Literacy course each year, we have included more lessons that explicitly teach students how to tackle difficult expository text used in their content-area classrooms, such as history, mathematics, and science. Still, our real challenge remains in helping students independently apply the knowledge they have gained in Academic Literacy to all their other academic courses. For our fourth year of Academic Literacy, we are planning to incorporate thematic units with collections of expository texts on focused themes, such as the History Detectives unit explored in *Reading for Understanding.* We plan to involve our colleagues in other departments in suggesting and gathering a range of types of texts for these units. It is our hope that our work with these units, combined with our continuing effort to implement literacy strategies across the curriculum, will give students the resources they need to negotiate challenging texts of any kind, from a biology textbook to the drivers' education manual.

4

The Voice Inside Your Head Asks, "Are You Comprehending?"

Carolyn Orta

Carolyn Orta teaches a sixth-grade social studies/language arts core class at Abbott Middle School in San Mateo, California. With two colleagues (one of them is Amy Smith, the author of Chapter Five in this book), she participated in the first National Institute on Reading Apprenticeship facilitated by the Strategic Literacy Initiative in 2000. She has gone on to implement Reading Apprenticeship approaches in her own classes and with work colleagues at Abbott Middle School on Reading Apprenticeship across the curriculum. In this chapter, she describes a lesson that engages students in making meaning of a poem by Thomas Lux, "The Voice You Hear When You Read Silently."

I am surveying the thirty sixth-grade students in front of me, giving each one the eagle eye. The class waits. They know the look. A collective anticipation hovers over the room. Hands on hips and shoulders back, I strut back and forth, through the maze of desks. Amanda's eyes twinkle; she wants to blurt the answer before the question is even posed. Mandy twirls her pencil and begins scanning the walls of the room for more interesting information. Danny sighs and drops his head on the desk. Finally, in fire-and-brimstone manner, the all-too-familiar question escapes my lips: "Okay, class, if you're not comprehending, then what?"

"You're not reading!" the class responds in unison.

"Where's your energy?" I demand. "Tell me again!"

"If you're not comprehending, you're not reading!" they shout even louder.

This is the scene in my sixth-grade social studies/language arts/reading core class midyear as we begin reading instruction for the day. "If you're not comprehending, you're not reading" has turned into a class mantra.

After teaching for a decade, primarily in middle school, grades 6 through 8, I am always on the prowl for ways to have my students understand that reading is a complex task and that unless they are engaged in the process of making meaning, they are simply looking at symbols and not reading at all. Students do not readily accept this concept. They focus only on getting the work done. Thus, they need frequent reminders as to what reading is: *the process of making meaning from text.* In addition to this mantra, the students, working in groups, have created metaphors for the reading process—for example:

- Reading is a puzzle—you have to put the pieces together to form the whole picture.

- Reading is a track race—you have to jump hurdles to get to the finish.

- Reading is a detective—you have to look for clues to solve the mystery.

Because I teach three subjects to the same group of students, I have the luxury of integrating the curriculum and teaching reading within a content area. I have also taught separate reading classes to seventh and eighth graders. However, I find that teaching reading comprehension is more effective when students apply what they learn to the content materials that they are expected to read and understand. I believe that every piece of written text, from a school lunch menu to a chapter in the social studies text, is an opportunity for students to explore the reading process. One such opportunity is

Thomas Lux's poem, "The Voice You Hear When You Read Silently." This poem shows students that reading is not only a complex task but also inextricably tied to our individual life experiences.

Beginning the Exploration of the Reading Process

I begin, as I usually do, by handing out copies of the text to the students. For this piece, we start out working as a whole class. I first ask, "What type of text are we looking at?" One student says it is a poem. I then ask, "Does anyone else agree?" The majority of the students raise their hands. Next, I ask, "What evidence do you have that the text is a poem?" Another student chimes in that it has to be a poem from the way the words are printed on the page. After confirming that the text is indeed a poem, I then ask students to make predictions about the poem based on the title: "The Voice You Hear When You Read Silently."

Although the students frequently make and write predictions in class, they have difficulty with this title. When such a situation arises, the students work with a partner, called their "Study Buddy," to discuss ideas together. Students are more willing to share with the class if they have talked with someone else first. Typical student predictions are, "I predict the poem is about someone reading aloud to you," "I predict the poem will be about reading to yourself," and "I have no idea what this poem is going to be about. The title doesn't make any sense!"

After students have some idea about the subject of the poem, I read the poem aloud to them with no instruction other than to follow along with their copy and listen. I want them to hear the piece from beginning to end with no interruption. This reading serves as an introduction, and students will get impatient if they are not allowed to hear the poem in its entirety. Also, I want to share with them that a poem is a text requiring many readings. For the second reading, students follow along and highlight words they do not understand. After the second reading, students share, first with partners and then with the whole class, words they do not know. We then survey the class to see if anyone has prior knowledge about the word in question to share with the class. Usually, someone will; however, if not, the person who highlighted the word will look it up in the dictionary and then share the definition with the class.

A typical exchange between the class and myself sounds like this: "Who has a word they don't understand? Yes, Tahni?"

"I don't understand what *cathedral* means."

"Okay, class, does anyone have prior knowledge with this term?"

Immediately, about three hands raise, one tentatively.

"Yes, Alex?

"I think it means some kind of church. When I was in Europe, we visited a lot of cathedrals."

"That's right. A cathedral is a type of church. Anyone have more information to add?"

"I think it's a really big church . . . really tall."

"Good, Garrett. That's usually true. Any other words?"

"I don't get *abstracts*."

Several more hands raise.

"Abstracts are like, remember when we write in our quote books and some of the quotes are literal and some are abstract? Abstracts are like it doesn't mean what the words say—it means something different."

"Good job, Erin. Any other words?"

"I don't know what *literary* means."

No hands go up.

"Class, no one has an idea about *literary*? Okay, let's see if we can work it through. Ever heard the word anywhere before?"

Silence.

"How about when we learn about literary terms."

"Oh, yeahs" buzz around the class. One or two hands fly up.

"Two people are making a connection. Good."

Two more hands go up. Whispers whip through the class, and several more hands go up.

"Suzanne, what do you think?"

"Well, *voice* is one of our literary terms, and the poem talks about literary sense and voice. So I think those ideas are related."

"Excellent. Great connection. So the poet is making a distinction between the literary term of voice and the sound of your own voice."

Now I tell the students their task is to work in groups of four, which I assign, to make sense of the rest of the text. I tell them the process will take time and remind them to use the context clues strategies we have been practicing all year. To demonstrate their efforts at making meaning from the text, each group will perform the poem, from memory, in front of the class.

Performing the Poem

In order to provide a model of the performance piece for them, I pull four students aside, give them the song "Row, Row, Row Your Boat," and show them how to interpret the lyric in a way different from the conventional meaning. Here is how the script went:

STUDENT 1 (fearfully): Row!
STUDENT 2 (fearfully): Row!
STUDENT 3 (fearfully): Row!
STUDENT 4 (threateningly): YOUR BOAT!
STUDENT 1 (terrified): G . . . G . . . Gently
STUDENT 2 (terrified): d . . . d . . . down
STUDENT 3 (terrified): th . . . th . . . the
STUDENT 4 (ominously): STREAM!
STUDENT 1 (timidly): merrily?
STUDENT 2 (timidly): merrily?
STUDENT 3 (timidly): merrily?
STUDENTS 1,2,3 in unison (timidly): merrily?
STUDENT 4 (growling): Life is but . . .
STUDENTS 1,2, 3 (in unison and suddenly relieved): A DREAM!

After the students practice the script, I interrupt the group work to show them the model. First, I hold up the lyrics to "Row, Row, Row Your Boat," written on a poster, and ask how many students know the song. Most do. I tell them we are going to sing it as a class for those who haven't heard it. We sing the song. Then I tell the students that simply by changing the emphasis and the pausing, we can change the meaning of the song. The four students then perform the new version, and we discuss how the meaning changed from a lazy summer day to waking up from a nightmare.

The "Row, Row, Row Your Boat" example is important in order to show the students another way, a physical way, to demonstrate the meaning of a text. The performance group Word for Word introduced me to the concept of using choral reading in this way. The group takes a piece of literature, usually a short story, and performs the work literally word for word. They use voice volume, pitch, tone, and body placement to convey the meaning of the story. They sometimes speak in unison or finish each other's sentences to place emphasis on certain parts of the text. In the "Row, Row, Row Your Boat" example, I point out to the kids that speaking the words "a dream!" in unison emphasizes the sense of relief the characters feel. I point out that emphasis, pausing, and the number of people speaking at one time can bring out a different meaning. I then give students three forty-five-minute class periods to work on breaking down the "Voice You Hear" poem, deciding how to perform it and practicing.

Students work all over: clustered around a coffee table, sprawled over bean bag chairs, sitting at desks or outside in the hallway. They consult dictionaries and write definitions on their copies of the poem. Sometimes they trust a group member's prior knowledge, and sometimes not.

"Hey, what's a 'haunches'?"

"I think it's some part of the cow . . . I think the feet."

"Are you sure?"

"Sort of."

"Let's look it up!"

"What do you think 'dark cathedral' means?"

"I think the cathedral means your brain, and dark because, well, it's dark in there. I think it means the tone of your voice in your brain."

In addition to writing out definitions, students highlight their parts and use underlines to denote emphasis or slash marks for pauses. With so many notations, the copies begin to get difficult to read. I provide students with a second copy to use for their final versions. One group, after unsuccessfully trying to read the title in unison, decides to read it in a round. Another group adds hand gestures, such as pointing to their heads or indicating quotation marks with their fingers. Yet another group adds props: a cassette tape is waved in the air with the words "the sound of a tape played back" and a flashlight goes on with the phrase "a sensory constellation is lit." Still another group decides to add a physical formation by lining up one behind the other and having the person talking "pop out." Each of these choices shows what the students are learning about the poem itself.

In places where no clear choices were made, such as the part that reads, ". . .your voice heard by an internal ear informed by internal abstracts and what you know by feeling, having felt," indicates to me that comprehension is probably weak in that section. I work with groups individually on this section, asking them questions and trying to pull ideas from them. When even the gifted students cannot figure it out, I realize this phrase is probably beyond their eleven years and decide it is not worth the effort to wrestle out the meaning of an idea beyond their experience.

Assessing Understanding

After the group performances, which are videotaped, I want to know if these activities have in fact brought the students closer to understanding the text. I ask them to respond in writing whether the meaning of the poem became clearer for them and what the poem means to them. Here are some of their efforts:

I think the poem means that when you are reading silently to yourself, you can hear a voice that no one else can ever hear. It is a different voice from the one you are used to. It says the word and then shows you a picture to go along with that word. But the picture it sends you is your picture. No one else has the same picture sent to them.   —Erin

The meaning of the poem became clearer to me because by helping other people memorize and emphasize their lines I was able to digest it. Also, how we read the poem made the meaning clearer to me. . . . I think the poem means that when we read to ourselves words aren't really words at all, they are feelings. Feelings of happiness, and hatred, sadness and acceptance, anger and love, that come with the words we read, but we feel different from one another after we read such words. For example, the word *cat*, you may think of how you love your cat Fluffy, but the person next to you may think of how they are allergic to cats.   —Suzanne

I think the poem means that wene you read to youre self you don't hear the voice of the person who rout it but yours.   —Reyes

I think it means that when you read, you are talking to yourself and you're not just reading words, you are listening to yourself, and that every word you read is a memory or experience you've had, reminds you of something, or your opinion of the world.   —Jenny

Some students said the stress of memorizing the poem interfered with their ability to comprehend the poem. Chelsea comments, "The poem didn't become clearer to me because I was so focused on trying to memorize the poem that I wasn't even concentrating on the poem."

I required students to memorize the poem to tie in with our social studies ancient history curriculum. We study how the *Vedas*, the collection of sacred hymns and poems that are the roots of the Hindu religion, are passed down orally from generation to generation because the Aryan people had no written language. I want the students to experience memorization firsthand.

More important, I want to give students yet another opportunity to grapple with text rather than make a cursory reading. I want them to jump into the messy mud puddle of reading and experience the richness of the process: to recognize the complexity of the task, delight in the texture of the language, taste the power of ideas, and create an entire world of meaning from a simple smear of ink.

The ultimate goal is to have our class mantra become embedded in consciousness as reflected in the words of another student, Garrett: "By breaking down the poem I understood it like I was the one who wrote it and I really got a clearer understanding."

5

Creating a Reading Apprenticeship Classroom

Amy Smith

Amy Smith teaches a seventh-grade social studies/language arts core class at Abbott Middle School in San Mateo, California. She has collaborated with Carolyn Orta (the author of Chapter Four in this book) and another colleague in her district to provide professional development for teachers at the school in Reading Apprenticeship across the curriculum. In this chapter, she describes how she uses Reading Apprenticeship approaches to help her students improve their comprehension of text in social studies.

My introduction to the Strategic Literacy Initiative's Reading Apprenticeship framework began when a colleague invited me to spend a week in Sonoma County, north of San Francisco, to learn about a program designed to help middle and high school students improve their reading comprehension. As a fairly new teacher, I was eager to explore new approaches and strategies to improve my classroom instruction. That week, I learned about the Reading Apprenticeship approach, which places the teacher in the role of a master, or more experienced, reader and the students in the role of "reading apprentices." I was attracted by the program's support and encouragement of students' taking responsibility for their own learning.

Over the following school year, my students and I developed into a community of readers as we shared our strategies for making sense of the different kinds of texts we read in studying seventh-grade social studies and literature. We also learned how to make the invisible process of reading visible. Here is my story of that school year.

Abbott Middle School, in a suburban city south of San Francisco, has over eight hundred students and more than forty staff members. The student population represents many different economic and ethnic backgrounds: African American, Asian, Caucasian, and Eastern European. My classes, two seventh-grade cores—a two-period block class that includes English and social studies—are made up of general education students, students who receive specialized academic support for one to three periods a day, and English language learners.

Making the Invisible Visible

Reading Apprenticeship instruction in my classroom begins in October during the English period of the core class with my students reading the poem "The Voice You Hear When You Read Silently" by Thomas Lux. I use this poem as an introduction because it sets the stage for two important Reading Apprenticeship concepts: that our personal life experiences have a powerful effect on the way we understand what we read and that the process of reading is invisible. After reading the poem, students respond to my questioning about what they feel the author is trying to say about reading.

"He is saying that we are reading in our heads," says one student.

Another adds, "I think he means we can all read the same thing, but everyone will maybe learn different things."

As we continue our conversation about the poem, the students are drawn to the lines that describe the barn. As they share their responses, I am struck by the varieties of experience my students have with the images the poem evokes.

One student remarks, "I have never seen a barn before."

Another responds, "I have—at my grandparents'. It's brown with two huge white doors. They keep hay and tools and stuff in it."

Someone who knows what a barn is will have a better understanding of the reference in the poem. All the life experience and education we bring into every learning situation helps us understand new concepts better. We discuss how important this is for our comprehension of all the texts we read. For the English language learners in my class, I stress that although they may not have experiences of all the words in the poem, everyone can add some associations from their cultures as part of our common understanding.

Continuing our discussion, students agree that reading occurs in our mind. I tell them that working with the ideas of Reading Apprenticeship will help us make the process of reading visible. Because of my experience as a reader, I will apprentice them in reading: I will show them what I am thinking when I read and what my brain tells me to do when I am not sure I understand a piece of text. I will also provide them with opportunities to investigate and share their own comprehension strategies with their classmates. Our reading goal for the year emerges from this discussion: all students will become aware of and able to use multiple strategies to gain comprehension of what they read.

In order to model Reading Apprenticeship strategies for my students and to get them comfortable with the process before extending their application to social studies and literature texts, I use the following selected readings from An Anthology for Reading Apprenticeship: "Coming into Language" by Jimmy Santiago Baca, an excerpt from John Steinbeck's "The Open Door," Gary Lee's interview, "Two Ways to Be a Warrior" about Luis Rodriguez, and "Tuning" by Gary Paulsen. Each author tells the story of how he overcame his personal struggle with reading. Some of these readings are more difficult than others and will require that the students share their understanding as we read them together. These readings also encourage students to talk freely about their own struggles with reading. Students are often surprised and seem relieved to learn that published writers may once have been unsuccessful students and readers. This is part of demystifying reading, an important part of Reading Apprenticeship.

Thomas Lux's poem introduces a set of key ideas we continue to discuss as we work with the next piece we use from the anthology, "Coming into Language" by Jimmy Santiago Baca. Lux's idea that each individual's reading is an invisible process is tied to his idea that we use our previous life experiences to understand text in our own unique ways.

Building Vocabulary

To tap into and reinforce students' prior knowledge, we review vocabulary words we have discussed before, such as *graveyard shift*, *Chicano*, *Anglo*, *vigilantes*, and *inarticulateness*. Before reading "Coming into Language," I introduce other words that are necessary for students to know in order to make meaning of this new text. Students are given this list and asked to write down the meaning of any of the words they know. Then they look up unknown words in the dictionary to find the part of speech and definition. Students write sentences using each word to show their understanding, and they share the sentences with the class. I encourage students to use context clues and the dictionary, or any other strategy, to discover word meanings of other difficult words we have not yet discussed, such as *mangled*, *revolt*, and *extradite*.

Capturing Reading Processes

To begin, I ask students to read silently a piece of text. When they have finished, I ask them several questions to discover what they did to make sense of the text:

- What strategies did you use to understand the text even if you were not explicitly aware of them at the time?

- What got in the way?

- What comprehension problems did you solve?

- What, if any, problems remain unsolved?

They also list any confusions that get in the way of their comprehension of the text, such as awkward column breaks or difficult vocabulary words that may make the text difficult to follow.

Students share the strategies they use to make sense of the reading as I write them on chart paper for all to see. Next, I ask them to list anything else that interfered with their understanding of the text, which could range from noise outside to difficult wording. Finally, they share the individual strategies they use to solve comprehension problems. If any comprehension problems are left unsolved, I offer my own strategies for students to try.

From this process, we create a "Good Reader Strategies" list using all the strategies from our class chart (see Exhibit 5.1). The strategies in this list become more complex as the students become more aware of the processes they go through to make sense of what they read. The list is posted permanently in front of the class, and we constantly refer to it to solve comprehension problems and add new strategies. We follow the same routine of capturing our reading processes for the remaining four reading selections because it creates a good base of general reading strategies that students can refer back to when they find themselves with comprehension problems they cannot solve. By the time we finish reading all five selections, students are well into Reading Apprenticeship.

Extending Reading Apprenticeship

To extend Reading Apprenticeship strategies into our social studies content, I begin with a textbook walk-through, focusing students' attention on the organization and format of the book. I point out the way this social studies book, like most other history textbooks,

Exhibit 5.1. Good Reader Strategies

- Reread.
- Look up definitions of words in the dictionary.
- Use the dictionary to find out how to say a word.
- Sound unknown words out.
- Use context clues to figure out hard words.
- Preread before reading the textbook. Look at titles, subtitles, key terms, pictures, and captions first.
- Bold words indicate a key term.
- Visualize or make mental pictures of what you are reading.
- Try to connect what you are reading to stuff you are personally interested in.
- Ask someone if you don't understand something after rereading.
- Use your prior knowledge or what you already know about the subject.
- Chunk the text by breaking reading into smaller sections to read.
- Review key terms, pictures, and captions after reading.
- A comma can indicate a definition.
- After you read, put the reading into your own words.
- Ask questions of the text.
- "Or a . . ." indicates a definition.
- Read in a quiet place.

is often organized to highlight cause and effect. As a more experienced reader in social studies, I am apprenticing my students by showing them some of the text features I pay attention to as I am reading. As they learn to look for and interpret these and other structures common to social studies, they become better able to look for and understand this common organizational format for historical texts.

In order to get students to apply their "good reader strategies" in social studies and to practice using these strategies as they read the textbook, I ask students to read the first five lessons for homework over the course of a week and complete a "Capturing Our

Reading Process" routine for each one. Having students carry out this now-familiar classroom routine on their own for homework and applying it to their social studies reading leads to good metacognitive conversation about our reading processes the next day. As we discuss what gets in the way of reading at home for students, what got in the way of comprehending the particular lessons in the textbook, and what is needed for students themselves to recognize their strategies and confusions, we are creating safe space to share confusions, reinforcing the strategies that good readers use, and coming up with new strategies to solve what got in the way at home. As we work through students' problems and strategies, we begin to establish that distractions such as fatigue, hunger, and noisy siblings really are excuses; students offer possible solutions to these specific problems such as "eating before studying" or "closing the door to where you study."

Using Metacognitive Logs

An important extension of metacognition is the application of metacognitive logs to social studies textbooks. At least once a week and with particularly challenging material, students are asked to focus in their logs on *how* they are reading the material rather than on its content. I ask students to think of themselves as scientists whose research subject is themselves. They observe themselves reading and then take notes on their reading process. This activity serves two purposes. It gives students practice in reflecting on their own reading processes with academic texts, helping them become more aware of what they do and do not do when they read. It also allows me to learn about the problems they encounter and the solutions they come up with as they read.

By writing in a metacognitive log, students become more aware of the strategies and the confusions they encounter as they try to comprehend difficult text. This gives them a better understanding of what they need to focus on figuring out. We start entries in class by using the prompts from *Reading for Understanding*, which include sentence starters such as "I got confused when . . .," "I started to think about . . .," and "I figured out that . . . ." In modeling as the more experienced reader, I share my responses to one or two of the prompts. After the students have had a chance to write their responses in their logs, we share our entries. Eventually, students move to doing the logs completely on their own.

I also use metacognitive logs with literature. I introduce *The Clay Marble* by Minfong Ho, a wonderful novel that takes place in the Cambodian refugee camps during the 1980s. It is about a young girl learning to believe in herself with the help of a very special friend amid the chaos of these turbulent times in Cambodia. In our metacognitive logs in literature, we respond to the prompt by adding a second part to it that asks students to *do* something to try to fix up their comprehension problems. For example, the prompt "I got confused when . . ." becomes "I got confused when . . . so I. . . ."

Before they begin reading the novel, students compile their own personal list of good reader strategies. For the first three chapters, we read and do the entries together in class so that I can model the problem-solving part of the prompt. After Chapter Three, students read silently and complete the entries on their own. For example, one student wrote, "While I was reading, I got confused when they were talking about the Vietnamese soldiers scaring the Khmer Rouge soldiers because I thought they were on the same side, so I reread and realized they were both trying to take control of Cambodia." Another wrote, "While I was reading, I was confused on a word so I looked it up in the dictionary."

Each day, we share from our metacognitive logs from the previous day before students begin reading. I ask for any confusions they are unable to solve. As a class, we share strategies to resolve the confusions and add new strategies to our class and personal good reader strategies list. I also use *The Clay Marble* to reinforce the cause-and-effect organization of text by having students search for events in the text and the effects resulting from these events.

Teaching Strategies

Throughout the Reading Apprenticeship work, I model the reading behavior I expect from my students by using the material they will be using. Modeling ensures that students know what is expected of them and gives them an example of how to make their confusions and strategies visible. It is the key to helping students develop flexible tools and resources for becoming more skilled and independent readers.

At the beginning, the teacher is the master reader. Modeling helps the students as apprentices take over with increasingly skillful use of the "tools of the craft" in the process of becoming master readers themselves. Students understand that although teachers and other adults struggle periodically with text, the strategic use of selected strategies can help them solve reading comprehension difficulties.

I continue to keep the Reading Apprenticeship discussion alive in my classroom. After students experience a new strategy, such as using context clues to get at the meaning of unknown words, I ask, "Could you use this in math or science?" Discussions are constantly occurring about using the strategies in other classes and how they benefit students' comprehension of what we read. These discussions always lead us back to our goal of becoming aware of and able to use multiple strategies to comprehend what we read.

Through focusing on how we are making meaning and solving comprehension problems that arise as we study social studies and literature, students build their capacity for reading more difficult texts more independently. As students work collaboratively, offering strategies to solve other students' confusions, they are learning new strategies from each other.

At the end of the year, a high-achieving student writes in his metacognitive journal, "The reading process analysis helps put what you've read on paper. When you write about what you are reading, the reading becomes easier to understand. When I use the strategies, it helps me become a better and more experienced reader. Anyone can read a book, but each one of us reads it differently."

By embedding the Reading Apprenticeship framework in my classroom and helping students identify and learn from those differences, those differences are making my classroom a livelier and richer home for learning.

6

Designing an Effective Academic Literacy Course

Ruth Schoenbach

In Chapter One, we introduced the pilot Academic Literacy course, our definition of academic literacy more broadly as it is embedded in subject-area classes, and a brief overview of the Reading Apprenticeship framework, which is the foundation of this work. Chapters Two through Five have presented detailed explorations of students and teachers who are developing the kinds of Reading Apprenticeship classroom environments that can lead to more engaged and strategic reading. Here we return to a discussion of the stand-alone Academic Literacy course described in *Reading for Understanding* and offer design guidelines in terms of structure, curriculum, and classroom interactions to guide other educators in creating effective Academic Literacy courses in their own settings.

Since the publication of *Reading for Understanding* in 1999, we have witnessed a proliferation of courses called Academic Literacy that cover a very wide range of curricular and course designs. Publication of *Building Academic Literacy: An Anthology for Reading Apprenticeship* and this companion book provides an opportunity to articulate some design guidelines that we believe will increase the likelihood of more students making significant—even, in many cases, dramatic—improvements in their academic literacy. We realize, even as we articulate these guidelines, that educators may be constrained in ways that will interfere with some of these recommendations. We offer guidelines here to describe what we believe

will result in the biggest gains for a wide range of students, particularly those who struggle with reading assigned academic texts.

Academic Literacy Course and Curriculum Design Guidelines

**The Academic Literacy course should be a seen
as a course for most or all ninth-grade students
to prepare them for rigorous academic reading and writing
across the disciplines, not as a "remedial" course**

As the positive results in the pilot Academic Literacy class described
in Chapter One suggest and as Lisa Messina and Elizabeth Baker
argue in Chapter Three, a wide range of students can benefit from
participation in an Academic Literacy course. A well designed Academic Literacy course can support, challenge, and engage students
from struggling readers to more able but disengaged readers, to avid
readers who can extend their range of reading expertise. As a result
of our experience, listening to stories of Academic Literacy classes
around the country and beginning to collect new data on student
outcomes, we believe that Academic Literacy classes that target students scoring in the bottom quartile on standardized tests are much
less successful than schools offering Academic Literacy as heterogeneous classes for all (or almost all) ninth-grade students.

**The curriculum for an Academic Literacy course
should provide students with opportunities to
explore a core set of ideas about literacy and
their own literacy identities using texts written
by a diverse group of authors in multiple genres**

The anthology that this book accompanies, *Building Academic Literacy: An Anthology for Reading Apprenticeship*, is designed as a resource
for such exploration. Selections in the anthology, written by a di-

verse group of authors, represent multiple genres: poems, directions, newspaper articles, and a variety of types of narrative and expository texts. All the selections in the anthology focus on a broad but powerful set of themes related to the content of Unit 1: Reading Self and Society. In addition, the readings have been chosen—and have been field-tested—with an eye toward providing a wide range of text styles and difficulty levels. To help teachers have a sense of the range of the difficulty of these selections, we have appended a "Readability Rating" of the selections from the anthology using the Degrees of Reading Power levels (see Appendix H). Nevertheless, we urge teachers to remember that readability formulas do not include intangible variables such as students' interest and background knowledge related to the various readings and to remember the limitations of readability formulas in general. Although word length, sentence length, and other measures can help teachers and students gauge text difficulty to a degree, they are not always good predictors of what texts students will find accessible.

The anthology selections in Part One: Literacy and Identity, offer students many points of exploration, identification, and difference. The links to the personal and social dimensions of the Reading Apprenticeship framework are powerful and can pull in even very reluctant readers. The second set of selections, Literacy and Power, address an aspect of Reading Apprenticeship's social dimension that we believe is especially critical for students who are skeptical about the value of literacy in their lives. The selections in Part Three, How We Read, address another topic central to the first unit of the Academic Literacy course. Students read and discuss these selections as they learn and practice a variety of strategies for making their own invisible processes of reading visible. A fourth core idea in Unit 1 of Academic Literacy is that different types of texts represent different discourse communities, each with particular ways of using language and structuring text. The selections in Part Four, Breaking Codes, present and explore a variety of discourse communities and types of texts ranging from comics to technical writing, from cinema to hip-hop.

An Academic Literacy course should integrate Silent Sustained Reading with metacognitive logs as a powerful key routine

Perhaps the most important part of this first unit is that students begin Sustained Silent Reading (SSR) of self-chosen books. In SSR, students read a book of their choice for twenty minutes at least twice a week. Students are expected to read at least two hundred pages each month, to maintain a reflective reading log (see Chapter Three of this book), to write reflective letters about their reading to the teacher, and to design a project or presentation about their book. Far from discouraging students from reading, the seriousness with which SSR is treated soon communicates to students the importance of reading and has the effect of reengaging those who had stopped reading as they moved into middle school.

A great deal of rigorous research has established that extensive reading builds knowledge of content as well as language and fluency.[1] This is especially important for students for whom English is not their first language. In addition, the element of choice in reading is very important in increasing students' intrinsic motivation for reading, which has been shown to be significantly related not only to their identity as readers but to their ability to tackle challenging texts.[2] Unfortunately, some recent misrepresentations of this body of research on SSR have led some educators to question the value of this practice, claiming that there is no research to support the value of Silent Sustained Reading for improving students' reading.[3]

We agree that SSR can be implemented poorly, resulting in students' "just turning pages" and pretending to read. Holding students accountable to the classroom community helps reinforce the seriousness of this aspect of the Academic Literacy course. When implemented well with routines for accountability, a focus on the reading process (through metacognitive logs,) and opportunities and expectations to share "book talk" with classmates in a variety of ways, SSR can be a key catalyst for students' increasing engagement, fluency, and confidence as readers.

The curriculum for an Academic Literacy course should be designed with routines for scaffolding students' strategic repertoire and increasing ability to use strategies appropriately and independently

Beginning with Unit 1 and continuing throughout the year, students are learning and practicing a variety of metacognitive, cognitive, text-wise, and knowledge-building strategies as they read selections about the core ideas and thematic topics that focus each unit. Teachers model strategies for students and provide guided practice to enable students to work in a variety of group structures (pair-share, small group, student-led whole group work, teacher-led whole group work, fishbowl.) Teachers plan deliberately to provide opportunities for students to become increasingly independent in their use of strategies.

The curriculum for an Academic Literacy course should both address and stretch beyond students' sphere of knowledge and experience

Scholar and high school English teacher Carol Lee has created and conducted research on an approach she calls "cultural modeling," in which African American students use their sophisticated, though often not explicit, knowledge of literary elements such as irony, foreshadowing, and subtext as they appear in popular culture, such as in songs or television commercials, to bridge into reading literature, which is further removed from their experience.[4] The same underlying idea—helping students recognize the complexity of what they already know how to do in their "reading" of the media—motivates the second unit of the Academic Literacy course.

Unit 2: Reading Media was designed as a six-week unit that introduces students to commercials as visual texts similar in some ways to printed texts. Students also read a challenging theoretical essay on the role of media in our understanding of experiences in which we cannot participate directly. Students learn to investigate texts as authors' creations devised or constructed in particular times and places with specific purposes, intended audiences, and points of view. Students learn about visual metaphors, symbolism, persuasive argument, key messages, casting, storyboard sketching, production notes, and targeted audiences. They carry out final projects that require them to analyze and then produce persuasive media pieces, using the elements they have been studying. Ideas on resources and curriculum design for this unit can be found in Appendix A.

The curriculum for an Academic Literacy course should be built around thematic units, using texts in varied genres and disciplines

Research on the explicit teaching of reading comprehension suggests that students are more likely to acquire and transfer reading comprehension strategies to new situations when they learn these strategies within a meaningful and coherent unit of study.[5] In addition, such thematic or topic-focused units offer students opportunities to build fluency and context knowledge as well as increasing confidence and motivation. Here we describe two such units in which students gain practice and confidence reading in history and in science: the Reading History unit created and taught in the pilot year of the Thurgood Marshall Academic Literacy course and the Reading Science and Technology unit created and taught at the school in the third year of the course.

Unit 3: Reading History was designed to help students put their personal experiences in a historical context by understanding the roots of modern issues of either immigration and social alienation or totalitarianism and aggression. The unit was designed to help students reconceptualize the discipline of history as an interpretive enterprise rather than an exercise in memorization. Students were assisted in developing a set of strategies to enable them to learn from a set of subject-area textbooks as well as primary source documents. They built background knowledge through extensive reading across a variety of topic-relevant texts, including modern films about historical events. For example, in exploring the topic of genocide in modern world history, students collected and read articles about current events in the Middle East and Africa, as well as reports of hate crimes in American cities. They read analyses of the social, historical, and psychological precursors and explanations for intergroup hostility and violence. They viewed historical documentaries about the Armenian genocide, as well as segments of *The Wave* and *Swing Kids*. *The Wave* is a film depicting the unintended and horrific outcome of an experiment in in- and out-group identity formation among teenagers, and *Swing Kids* is a film set in Nazi Germany as a group of jazz-loving teenagers comes of age and is forced to make choices, taking on or resisting roles in Germany's increasingly totalitarian and genocidal society.

Finally, as a culminating unit, students assumed the role of historian in an investigative project centered on the Holocaust. Working in groups and with both primary and secondary source documents related to a specific event such as the Warsaw ghetto uprising or the evolution of anti-Semitic laws in Germany, students interpreted and analyzed and finally presented their historical analyses of the event they had investigated.

Academic Literacy course teachers at Marshall designed Unit 4: Reading Science and Technology using the same curriculum design of the Reading History unit. This unit is also coherently focused, with a variety of texts addressing a central topic. The group of teachers who developed this unit chose the topic "Extreme Weather" to build on the base of knowledge students had from the earth science course they were taking concurrently.

When teachers are already so pressed for time, finding resources to develop curriculum units can seem like a daunting task. To minimize the burden, this group of four teachers divided responsibility, each finding texts on one of the subtopics: hurricanes, tornadoes, volcanoes, and earthquakes. Their primary source was the Internet, especially the U.S. Geological Survey Web site (http://pubs.usgs.gov) and the Discovery Channel's site (www.discovery.com). Other Web sites that can be helpful for educators wanting to develop thematic or topic-focused units in science and technology are the Web sites of the National Association of Science Teachers and the American Academy for the Advancement of Science. The Unit Curriculum overview in Appendix A includes these as well as other Web sites educators can use as starting points for finding resources for the Media Literacy and Reading History units.

Classroom Interactions

Academic Literacy classrooms should foster conversations focused on comprehension as well as on content

The work of comprehending reading materials takes place in the classroom; the teacher scaffolds the learning and serves as model and guide. This work is metacognitive; *how* readers make sense of text is as important as what sense they make of it.

Teachers should beware of these common pitfalls:

- Teachers may ask students to carry out metacognitive routines such as "talking to the text" but overlook modeling the routine themselves in the context of various reading activities.

- Teachers may model metacognitive conversation about texts but not provide students with sufficient opportunities to practice internal and external metacognitive conversations themselves.

A climate of collaboration and curiosity about everyone's thinking should be developing in an Academic Literacy classroom

Class members draw on each other's knowledge, serving as resources to make sense of text together. They respect and value problem-solving processes; classroom norms support risk taking, sharing knowledge and confusion, and working together to solve comprehension problems.

Grouping arrangements support collaboration and inquiry, with students working independently, in pairs, in small groups, and as a class, depending on the task and the text. A shared vocabulary to describe reading processes and text features is evident in classroom talk, materials in use, and materials on display.

Teachers should beware of these common pitfalls:

- Teachers may focus on the cognitive and knowledge-building dimensions of Reading Apprenticeship but overlook the crucial social and personal dimensions of Reading Apprenticeship.

- Teachers may feel insecure moving out of the typical teacher-to-whole-class discussion, question, and practice mode to give students carefully structured and phased-in practice working on reading comprehension in pairs and small groups.

- Teachers may ask all the questions rather than developing students' capacity to ask their own questions.

Student independence should be deliberately nurtured and supported in an Academic Literacy classroom

Students are agents in the process of reading and learning; they actively inquire into text meaning, their own and others' reading processes, the utility of particular reading strategies, and their preferences, strengths, and weaknesses as readers. They are expected and supported to read extensively; course-related materials are available on various levels, and accountability systems are in place to ensure that students read large amounts of connected text. Over time, students are expected and able to do more reading, make more sophisticated interpretations, and accomplish more work with texts with less support from the teacher during class time.

Teachers should beware of these common pitfalls:

- Teachers may believe that students who are struggling readers (that is, unable to independently comprehend grade-level texts) are not capable of sophisticated and independent work; they may not "trust" them to take on more responsibility for their own learning.

- Teachers may not be able to gather sufficiently diverse texts to enable students to exercise choice over reading materials and to read extensively in their classrooms. School libraries may have few resources to supplement classroom libraries.

- Teachers may not know how to plan for providing students with significant opportunities and guided practice in identifying their habits, thinking patterns, confusions, likes, and dislikes in relation to the texts they read, thus not providing students with the opportunity to develop increasing independence and sophistication as self-directed, self-motivated strategic readers.

- Teachers may not know how to choose texts at appropriate levels or to structure and set tasks at appropriate levels, with sufficient support and sufficient challenge, to enable students to work more and more independently.

Structure, Context, and Schoolwide Design Guidelines

An Academic Literacy course should be part of schoolwide work on reading and writing across the disciplines

In schools where staff have integrated a focus on literacy into subject-area classes, the benefits of a stand-alone ninth-grade Academic Literacy class are significantly amplified. Subject-area teachers have the benefit of not having to introduce students to key strategic routines used by active readers, because students have already been introduced to these in their Academic Literacy courses. At the same time, as subject-area teachers ask students to use these routines in their science, history, literature, math, or even shop classes, students gain important practice transferring these strategies to new situations. For this to occur, teachers in other content areas should be introduced to and supported in learning to include reading in their disciplines as an integral part of thinking and learning in their disciplines. Chapter Nine of *Reading for Understanding* provides guidance for this kind of on-site professional development.

Teachers who teach Academic Literacy should have time to explore the ideas and practices described in *Reading for Understanding* before beginning to teach the course

For teachers to create the kind of classroom community of inquiry into reading that is the core of an Academic Literacy class as we designed it, they need opportunities to understand and explore the underlying ideas of the Reading Apprenticeship framework, and—crucially—to practice using the metacognitive strategies at the heart of this approach with texts they find challenging. Again, Chapter Nine, Professional Development: Creating Communities of Master Readers, is a valuable resource.

Academic Literacy should be a year-long course

Developing increased fluency and internalizing a more active and strategic repertoire for reading a widening range of texts takes time and practice. Our experience indicates that a year-long Academic Literacy course is much more likely to have the kind of beneficial impact described in the pilot course than will a semester version.

Academic Literacy courses should involve community members to increase students' connections to and sense of purpose for work on reading

Efforts such as forming book groups that involve parents, students, and teachers, or arranging classroom visits by community members who discuss how the types of reading and writing they encounter in their daily work and personal lives are time-consuming but high-leverage activities which can significantly deepen students' sense of connection to literacy.

Final Thoughts and New Directions

Having described what we believe are the most critical elements for the success of an Academic Literacy course, we want to reiterate that we understand that there are many situations in which educators are not able to fully implement what we describe here as best practice. A variety of political, economic, and social factors constrain educators at all levels. Nevertheless, providing academically under-performing adolescents access to a rich and rigorous literacy learning environment, can have a tremendous personal and social payoff worth the effort it takes to work around these constraints as creatively as we can.

In the three years between the publication of *Reading for Understanding* and the writing of this book, there have been many excellent books written for educators interested in improving adolescent literacy. We point readers to some of them in the Bibliography. In these same three years, we have worked with hundreds of educators around the country who are breaking new ground in adolescent literacy. From Alaska to Arizona, Boston to Binghamton, Trenton, New Jersey to Chattanooga, Tennessee, innovative educators are finding new ways to nourish a next generation of readers, writers, and thinkers who help us and others see beyond today's constraints to futures we cannot yet imagine.

Appendix A
Academic Literacy Four-Unit
Curriculum Matrix

Unit	Focus	Key Activities	Readings	Reading, Speaking and Listening, and Writing Competencies
Unit 1: Reading Self and Society (approximately 12 weeks)	• Explore and broaden students' understandings of what reading is and where reading happens in their lives • Begin to build fluency, engagement, and vocabulary through Silent Sustained Reading (SSR) • Create community and connections building personal and social dimensions • Begin the metacognitive conversation	• Why read? (RfU, p. 59) Personal reading history map (LRA, Chap. 3) *Practicing metacognition* • Think-aloud with Play-Doh and with texts (LRA, Chap. 2) • Metacognitive Bus (RfU, pp. 57–58) • Capturing Our Reading Process/Good Readers' Strategies List (LRA, Chap. 5) • Begin SSR and metacognitive logs and learning to choose books you like (RfU, pp. 63–70) • Begin work on reciprocal teaching (optional) with "RT fishbowl" (LRA, Chap. 2)	• Selections from *Building Academic Literacy: An Anthology for Reading Apprenticeship*	• Learning to choose books that are both interesting and at students' independent reading level • Setting goals for individual reading improvement in terms of range of texts, fluency, and comprehension • Learning to notice and name reading processes used to comprehend texts • Working in pairs and small groups to increase comprehension of texts • Sharing reading processes and insights through metacognitive conversation • Writing SSR log entries and reflections on goals and growth as reader

Unit	Focus	Key Activities	Readings	Reading, Speaking and Listening, and Writing Competencies
Unit 2: Reading Media (approximately 6 weeks)	• Texts as constructions for particular audiences and purposes • Techniques of persuasion used in media texts • Visual metaphors, icons, symbolism	• Practice chunking (RfU p. 55) challenging expository text on media literacy • Practice reciprocal teaching with this same or similar text on media literacy • Analyze ads, looking for techniques of persuasion and visual metaphors, icons, and symbolism • Working in groups, create an ad using specific techniques of persuasion and visual metaphors, icons, and symbolism, targeted to a specific audience	• A variety of types of written and electronic texts in the broad area of media literacy • Some relevant texts may be found through the following Web sites: www.medialit.org, www.media-awareness.ca, www.nmec.org	• Identifying schema required by variety of types of texts • Identifying intended audiences and purposes of texts • Actively participating in RT discussion groups, taking each of the roles • Writing SSR log entries and reflections on goals and growth as reader

Unit	Focus	Key Activities	Readings	Reading, Speaking and Listening, and Writing Competencies
Unit 3: Reading History (approximately 10 weeks)	• Reconceptualize the discipline of history as an interpretive enterprise rather than an exercise in memorization	• News portfolio project (RfU, p. 113) • History Detectives project (see RfU, pp. 114–116) • Graphic organizers: Trees of Knowledge (RfU, p. 110) • In SSR, for extra credit, students are invited to read from a list of books related to the theme; students reading the same book can form book circles • Text modeling with different genres of historical primary and secondary source documents	• Textbook chapter, as overview and background • Primary source and secondary documents organized in thematically linked sets of texts • Some relevant texts may be found through the following Web sites: www.socialstudies.org, www.4teachers.org/ projectbased/	• Exploring a historical topic in depth while applying reading strategies learned in earlier units • Identifying features of different genres of texts read in history unit • Writing texts modeled on several of these genres (persuasive letter, textbook unit introduction, public notice)

Unit	Focus	Key Activities	Readings	Reading, Speaking and Listening, and Writing Competencies
Unit 4: Reading Science and Technology (approximately 8 weeks)	• Reconceptualize the discipline of science as a constantly developing field of knowledge rather than a set of static information.	• Science Detectives project, modeled on History Detectives project • Graphic organizers: Trees of Knowledge • In SSR, for extra credit, students are invited to read from a list of books related to the theme; students reading the same book can form book circles • Text modeling with different genres of scientific primary and secondary source documentst	• Textbook chapter, as overview and background • Primary source and secondary documents organized in thematically linked sets of texts • Some relevant texts may be found through the following Web sites: http://pubs.usgs.gov, www.discovery.com, www.actionbio science.org	• Exploring a scientific topic in depth while applying reading strategies learned in earlier units • Identifying features of different genres of texts read in science unit • Writing texts modeled on several of these genres (description of a process, newspaper report on new discovery, textbook unit introduction)

Note: RfU: Schoenbach, R., Greenleaf, C., Cziko, C., and Hurwitz, L. *Reading for Understanding: A Guide to Improving Reading in Middle and High School Classrooms.* San Francisco: Jossey-Bass, 1999. LRA: Lessons from Reading Apprenticeship Classrooms.

Appendix B
Academic Literacy Course Time Line: Embedding Routines Across the Year

September	October	November	December	January	February	March	April	May	June

Unit 1: Reading Self and Society   Unit 2: Reading Media   Unit 3: Reading History   Unit 4: Reading Science and Technology

Inquiry into self as reader, assessment, and evaluation of reading strategies, sharing with classroom community through talk and written reflections

Finding and assessing books using the "10-page chance"

Sustained silent reading (SSR) of a 200-page book per month

SSR logs with metacognitive writing about reading process

Thinking aloud, thinking on paper, talking about the process of making sense of texts

Activating background knowledge, building schema

Questioning strategies (QAR, ReQuest)

Approaching unknown words (using context cues, assessing familiarity, analyzing word parts)

Summarizing

Predicting using text signals

Clarifying (rereading, reading on)

Reciprocal teaching procedure

Chunking (parsing) complex sentences

Analyzing rhetorical appeals, symbolism, construction of media and texts

Previewing and prereading a text

Paraphrasing

Graphic organizers, tree diagrams

Locating main ideas in exposition

Interpreting primary sources

Appendix C
Academic Literacy in English
Course Description

This appendix provides the larger curriculum context for the parts of Daniel Moulthrop's course described in Chapter Two.

Academic Literacy in English   **San Lorenzo High School**
Instructor: Daniel Moulthrop

Course Description

How does reading happen? And how do we make ourselves into more effective, thoughtful, metacognitive* readers? This course is the foundation of the English department at San Lorenzo High School. Required of all students in the fall term of ninth grade, the course focuses on the development of reading strategies that will help students negotiate their way through all levels of literary study. Fundamentally, it is about reading and reflecting on reading through speech and writing.

Weeks 1–4: Reading Self and Society

We will read many different types of texts by a variety of figures both famous and not so famous. The works focus on the experience of reading and the roles literacy plays in intellectual, emotional, and social development.

---

*metacognitive (adj.) marked by an ability to think about your own thinking

Major assignments: Two Socratic seminars, a persuasive essay, reflective journals.

Goals: Students will begin the classroom conversation about metacognition and practice metacognitive behaviors, such as making connections to schema, questioning, thinking aloud, and Talking to the Text.

Weeks 5–9: *The House on Mango Street* by Sandra Cisneros

Major assignments: Two Socratic seminars, writing portfolio containing poetic and artistic responses to the text, as well as reflective journals and a reflective essay.

Goals: Students will continue to practice metacognitive behaviors and transfer skills learned in Self-Selected Reading to a classroom text. Students will also learn Reciprocal Teaching.

Weeks 10–14: Current Controversial Issues

We will practice our reading strategies and skills with nonfiction texts that deal with contemporary controversial issues.

Major assignments: Reciprocal Teaching, persuasive essay, debate (oral presentation).

Goals: Students will practice metacognitive reading strategies with expository texts, becoming expert "reciprocal teachers."

Weeks 15–18: Poems and Short Stories

We will finish up by enjoying some of the finest short stories and poems recently written.

Major assignments: Socratic seminars, Reciprocal Teaching, reflective journals.

Goals: Students will hone their metacognitive reading abilities by practicing with poems and short fiction, preparing them for the final exam, focused on Talking to the Text and Reciprocal Teaching.

Self-Selected Reading is also a major part of your grade. We will read in class every week, and you are also expected to read independently at home. In addition to the assignments listed here, there will be daily classwork and homework assignments involving reading and responses to what we read. We will also spend some class time on grammar (the basics on how to write).

At the end of this course, you will be able to . . .

- Select and complete a novel (or several) of your choice, independently reading a total of 500 pages every nine weeks.

- Reciprocal Teach (RT) an unfamiliar text (RT is a group reading process involving clarifying, summarizing, questioning, and connecting).

- Participate in Socratic seminars (discussion activity centered on questions written by students).

- Comprehend an unfamiliar text and demonstrate this understanding by "talking to the text," "thinking aloud," and producing a written summary.

- Metacognitively reflect on your own learning and reading.

- Demonstrate an understanding of audience and identify an author's purpose.

- Write descriptive paragraphs and essays modeled on the work of professional writers.

- Employ the skills and habits of successful high school students (cooperating with classmates, being prepared for class, taking responsibility for your own actions, contributing to your classmates' learning by sharing and participating).

Appendix D
Academic Literacy, Unit Three
Reading History

Those who do not study history are condemned to repeat it.

Santayana

Theme: Making Peace and Justice

This unit will focus on preparing students to take charge of their future by understanding the historical roots of modern problems, by connecting history to their personal lives, and by considering and posing solutions to current world problems that they will face, and be responsible for solving, as adults.

Thematically linked texts will focus either on Immigration and Migration Experiences or on Totalitarianism and Aggression in the Modern World, as the teacher chooses.

Goals

The primary goal of this unit is to assist students in developing a powerful set of strategies for *reading to learn* from a set of academic subject-area texts.

Developing Reading to Learn Strategies

The key strategies to be introduced and/or practiced during this unit include:

- Planning, or preparing for learning by developing good study habits

- Surfacing prior knowledge about a topic when approaching a new text

- Previewing a text to anticipate and organize learning from the text

- Reciprocal teaching or other active reading strategies including summarizing, questioning, clarifying, and predicting

- Locating and extracting key points and supporting details from a text

- Paraphrasing key quotations to render ideas in their own language

- Critically responding to the information and concepts in a text

Developing Word Knowledge

As a part of the introductory activities, students will begin to study word roots, prefixes, and suffixes as well as commonly used academic signal words. Teachers should also begin developing semantic networks associating many different words connected to the theme of the unit, whether immigration or aggression.

Developing Historical Knowledge

To prepare students specifically for further learning in history/social studies, each classroom should have a world map to assist with geographical concepts basic to understanding the modern world. In addition, each teacher should work with the students to create and elaborate a visible classroom time line to develop a better sense of the chronology of modern events.

Developing Research Skills

Finally, some attention to researching a topic, including locating resources and applying strategies of excerpting, paraphrasing, and responding to these research materials, will help develop students' beginning-level research skills.

Texts

Core texts for this unit *must* include *significant amounts of textbook material* to help students develop strategies for learning from these common academic texts. *In addition*, students will read primary texts, newspapers, narratives, Internet documents, video documentaries, political art, and other ancillary materials. To ensure that all students have an opportunity to practice the strategies for reading to learn, the class will read the majority of these texts together, as a whole class. In this way, students will have ample demonstration and practice with these strategies before they break into smaller groups or individual work for projects.

Core Activities

Silent Sustained Reading (SSR)	February, continue as before.
	March, invite students to read from a list of books related to the theme for extra credit; begin book conversations on the theme across the books students have read.
Reciprocal teaching (RT)	Continue and develop students' skill with the RT dialogue procedure, beginning, for example, with texts on planning and studying by Mel Levine.
	Continue using the RT procedure and/or key strategies of summarizing,

questioning, clarifying, and predicting through all texts assigned
for the unit.

Graphic Organizers

Trees of Knowledge: For each text read, students will individually, in groups, and in the whole class create visual summaries
of the information contained in the text, as follows. The *roots*
are prior knowledge about the topic that students have, even if
erroneous (not all roots survive), based on brainstorming, conversation, "Give One, Get One",[1] and others. The *trunk* is the
topic of the text from the title or teacher presentation. The
main branches are based on a preview of the text, the main
points to be covered in the text, labeled identically as the
main headings. The *smaller branches, twigs, and leaves* are based
on actually reading, RT style, and filling in the details to put
the foliage on the ideas.

Triple-entry journals: For each text read, students will
complete a triple-entry journal extracting (1) quotations
that state the main ideas, (2) their own paraphrase of these
quotations, and (3) their own response to these ideas. For
instance:

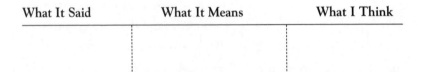

What It Said	What It Means	What I Think

The teacher might want to choose which quotations students
should paraphrase and respond to for particular texts. Students
will need to learn how to paraphrase in complete sentences,
perhaps even going "chunk by chunk" through the original
quotation.

Explicit attention should be drawn to paraphrasing as "putting into your own words, in your own language, in your own thoughts," drawing the distinction between this and "copying from the text" or "plagiarizing." This is what teachers mean when they say, "Use your own words."

Explicit attention could also be paid to how to quote and cite an original text, if desired. This is the reverse of paraphrasing, or putting things in your own words.

Final Project or Demonstration of Learning

The culmination of this unit is left up to teacher discretion, with a general guideline of the following: demonstrating the ability to locate, extract, summarize, and react to information contained in texts is more important, as it meets the goal for this unit, than a polished, final report. Some ideas teachers have considered include:

- An "I" Search, focused on the process of researching a topic related to the theme of the unit, put together as a journal, a log, or a scrapbook of learning

- Small group inquiries into a topic related to the theme (this must include some individual demonstration of mastery of the reading to learn strategies)

Appendix E
Student Reading Survey

Name _____ Teacher Name _____
School/Class _____ Grade _____ Date _____

1. What do you usually do when you read? (Check ALL the ones that describe what you do.)

☐ I read silently

☐ I try to figure out the meaning of words I don't know

☐ I look over what I'm going to read first to get an idea of what it is about

☐ I read aloud to myself in a quiet voice

☐ I look up words I don't know in the dictionary

☐ I picture what is happening in the reading

☐ I try to pronounce all the words correctly

☐ I get distracted a lot while I'm reading

☐ I ask myself questions about what I'm reading

☐ I try to read with expression

☐ I have trouble remembering what I read

☐ I put what I'm reading into my own words

☐ I try to get the reading over with as fast as I can

☐ I try to understand what I read

☐ I read a section again if I didn't understand it at first

☐ I try to read   ☐ I try to concentrate   ☐ I think about
   smoothly   on the reading   things I know
                                                            that connect
                                                            to the reading

☐ I do different
   things. It depends
   on what I'm
   reading

2. Why do you think people read? _____

_____

_____

_____

3. What do you think someone has to do to be a good reader?
   (Check ONLY the 3 most important ones.)

☐ read aloud well   ☐ enjoy reading   ☐ understand what
                                                   they read

☐ read with   ☐ read a lot   ☐ concentrate on
   expression   the reading

☐ pronounce all the   ☐ read harder books   ☐ know when they
   words correctly   are having trouble
                                                   understanding

☐ know the   ☐ read different kinds   ☐ use strategies to
   meaning of most   of books   improve their
   of the words   understanding

☐ read fast   ☐ other: _____

4. Do you think you are a good reader?   ☐ Yes   ☐ No
   ☐ It depends
   Explain why. _____

_____

_____

_____

5. Do you think you will read once you graduate from high school?   ☐ Yes   ☐ No
If so, what kinds of things do you think you'll read?

_____

_____

_____

6. Do you read in a language other than English? (If no, go on to question 7.)
If yes, which language(s)_____
In which language do you read best?_____

7. What kinds of things do you read OUTSIDE of school? (Check ALL the things you read.)

☐ newspapers   ☐ letters or e-mail   ☐ comic books   ☐ Web pages

☐ short stories   ☐ magazines   ☐ song lyrics   ☐ computer manuals

☐ novels   ☐ poetry   ☐ religious books   ☐ how-to books

☐ video game books or magazines   ☐ nothing   ☐ other (explain)

8. How *often* do you read something that is NOT a school assignment?

☐ every day   ☐ frequently   ☐ sometimes   ☐ not often   ☐ never

9. How *often* do you read at home FOR school assignments?

☐ every day   ☐ frequently   ☐ sometimes   ☐ not often   ☐ never

10. During the past 12 months, how many *books* have you read? How many of these were NOT for school?_____

11. What kinds of *books* do you like to read? (Check ALL the ones you like to read)

☐ science fiction   ☐ adventure/action   ☐ poetry   ☐ short stories

☐ thrillers   ☐ true life drama   ☐ romance   ☐ fantasy/myth

☐ picture books   ☐ comic books   ☐ science/nature   ☐ (auto)biography

☐ how-to books   ☐ sports   ☐ teen issues   ☐ humor

☐ history   ☐ horror   ☐ mysteries   ☐ none

☐ other _____

12. Who are your favorite authors? (List as many as you'd like.)

_____

_____

13. How do you choose a book to read? (Check ALL the ones that describe what you do.)

☐ look for an interesting title

☐ see how long the book is

☐ ask a teacher or librarian

☐ look at the pictures on the cover or in the book

☐ pick a book that looks easy

☐ ask a family member

☐ look to see if it has gotten an award

☐ look for a particular author

☐ ask a friend or classmate

☐ read the book cover or jacket

☐ look for books on a particular topic

☐ look in special displays at the library or book store

☐ read a few pages

☐ look for books I've heard about

☐ pick the Oprah Book Club selection

☐ look for particular kinds of books (dramas, horror, etc.)

☐ look for books that have been made into movies

☐ look for books about my culture

☐ I have no method of choosing a book

☐ other (describe) _____

14. Do you ever talk with a friend about something you have read?
    ☐ frequently   ☐ sometimes   ☐ never

15. Do you ever talk with a family member about something you have read?
    ☐ frequently   ☐ sometimes   ☐ never

16. Do you borrow from or trade books with friends or family members?
    ☐ frequently   ☐ sometimes   ☐ never

17. In general, how do you feel about reading? _____

    _____

    _____

    _____

    _____

Thank you for completing this survey.
I will use your answers to help guide my teaching.

_____

Adapted from Nancy Atwell[1]

Appendix F
Academic Literacy
Student Competencies

Area of Competency	Examples of What Students Will Know and Be Able to Do
Personal dimension	• Become increasingly aware of preferences, habits, processes, and growth as readers • Set goals for purposeful engagement with reading • Increase reading fluency • Increase confidence, risk taking, focus, and persistence in reading
Social dimension	• Share confusions about texts with others • Share successful processes and approaches to understanding texts with others • Participate in small- and large-group discussions about reading and texts • Appreciate alternative points of view
Cognitive dimension	• Monitor comprehension • Ask different types of questions of the text • Summarize the text • Clarify understanding of the text by rereading, searching for context clues, continuing to read, and tolerating uncertainty • Make predictions based on the content or structure of the text
Knowledge-building dimension: Content	• Use a variety of strategies to access and interpret information in textbooks and other course materials

Area of Competency	Examples of What Students Will Know and Be Able to Do
	• Preread texts and generate questions • Use graphic organizers to organize and build knowledge structures • Identify and access relevant knowledge and experiences
Knowledge-building dimension: Texts	• Identify text features such as signal words, structure, and specialized vocabulary • Approach novel words strategically, using prior experience, context, and structural clues to meaning • Identify and use structural signal words and phrases
Knowledge-building dimension: Disciplines and discourses	• Recognize the large questions, purposes, and habits of mind that characterize specific academic disciplines • View texts as constructed artifacts that are addressed to readers familiar with the worlds they represent • Become familiar with specialized vocabulary, semantics, concepts, phrases, idioms of different disciplines and discourses
Writing	• Write from a particular point of view • Respond to text excerpts • Paraphrase texts • Compose a variety of texts for different purposes (interviews, reflections, summaries, letters, descriptions, logs, commercials, journals, posters, oral presentations)
Research	• Categorize, synthesize, and organize information from texts • Evaluate information sources • Identify primary and secondary sources • Interpret primary source documents

Appendix G
Degrees of Reading Power
Test of Reading Comprehension

To evaluate the impact of the pilot Academic Literacy course on student reading development in 1996–1997, the SLI research team wanted to measure changes in student reading processes. The team also wanted the assessment to demand little from teachers in the way of time, while yielding information useful in instructional decision making. In lieu of conducting a controlled experimental design study, the SLI research team sought a norm-referenced test that would measure ninth-grade student performance and progress against that of a larger national population of students. The Degrees of Reading Power (DRP) test by Touchstone Applied Science Associates (TASA) came closest to meeting these criteria.

The DRP test measures student reading achievement. This test gives teachers information about students' reading levels that they can use in selecting or deciding how to teach grade-level texts, as well as provide information about students' performance in relation to a national sample of students. The DRP is based on a modified cloze procedure. Cloze passages, in which words are left out to be supplied by the reader, are a widely used technique for quickly determining the difficulty level of passages. Unlike most other standardized reading tests, the DRP focuses on how well students can construct meaning during reading rather than measuring, through multiple-choice answers, what students comprehend about the passage after reading. Omitted words are all common words even if the passage is difficult; thus, failure to respond correctly should indicate failure to comprehend the passage rather than failure to understand the response options. The test is constructed to eliminate the likelihood that guessing or other nonreading activities can be used to generate correct responses.

Student performance on DRP tests is reported on a readability scale (the DRP unit scale) that describes the most difficult text the student is expected to read with different levels of comprehension. The DRP readability scale indexes the relative proportion of common or frequently used words in the text, the relative proportion of short to long words in the text, and the relative length and complexity of sentences in the text. A mathematical formula based on the Bormuth mean cloze readability formula combines these features to predict the difficulty (readability) of a text. Touchstone Applied Sciences Associates has applied the DRP readability index to a variety of popular textbooks as well as common literature at all grade levels. In addition, it has measured the readability of trade publications for reading audiences of various ages. These measures of text difficulty for particular types of text provide real-world anchors for the interpretation of student performance on the DRP. Readability indexes are admittedly flawed as measures of text difficulty. Notably, they omit measures of text difficulty having to do with the reader's interest or background knowledge relevant to the topic of text passages. However, they do give a standard against which student reading ability can be measured. They provide some instructional information useful to a teacher regarding the kinds of texts students may be able to read with various degrees of comprehension. Student raw scores are converted to DRP scores and reported in DRP units and can be easily converted to national percentiles and normal curve equivalent scales for statistical comparisons.

Appendix H
Degrees of Reading Power
Readability Index
for Anthology Selections

In Appendix G we briefly discussed why we have chosen the Degrees of Reading Power (DRP) test as a standardized measure of reading comprehension. In this appendix, we offer the "readability" ratings that DRP has given the text selections included in *Building Academic Literacy: An Anthology for Reading Apprenticeship*. At the same time that we are offering these ratings, we want to emphasize that other factors such as topic knowledge and interest will greatly affect the in-practice "readability" of a text in practice.

The following one-page graphic presents an overview of TASA's DRP readability system, with examples of the correspondences between DRP readability ratings and a variety of well-known texts.

Following this overview, readers will find several pages that present the anthology selections in the order they appear in the anthology, with their corresponding DRP readability ratings.

Readers seeking more in-depth information on the DRP readability ratings system can find it through the TASA Web site (www.tasa.com).

The following information applies to the materials on the following six pages:

DRP Scale of Readability

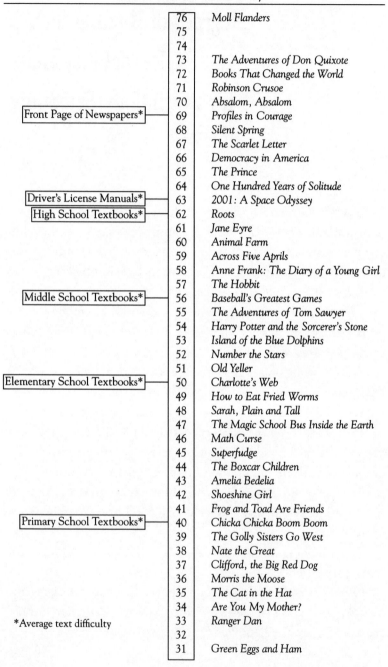

76	Moll Flanders
75	
74	
73	The Adventures of Don Quixote
72	Books That Changed the World
71	Robinson Crusoe
70	Absalom, Absalom
Front Page of Newspapers* — 69	Profiles in Courage
68	Silent Spring
67	The Scarlet Letter
66	Democracy in America
65	The Prince
64	One Hundred Years of Solitude
Driver's License Manuals* — 63	2001: A Space Odyssey
High School Textbooks* — 62	Roots
61	Jane Eyre
60	Animal Farm
59	Across Five Aprils
58	Anne Frank: The Diary of a Young Girl
57	The Hobbit
Middle School Textbooks* — 56	Baseball's Greatest Games
55	The Adventures of Tom Sawyer
54	Harry Potter and the Sorcerer's Stone
53	Island of the Blue Dolphins
52	Number the Stars
51	Old Yeller
Elementary School Textbooks* — 50	Charlotte's Web
49	How to Eat Fried Worms
48	Sarah, Plain and Tall
47	The Magic School Bus Inside the Earth
46	Math Curse
45	Superfudge
44	The Boxcar Children
43	Amelia Bedelia
42	Shoeshine Girl
41	Frog and Toad Are Friends
Primary School Textbooks* — 40	Chicka Chicka Boom Boom
39	The Golly Sisters Go West
38	Nate the Great
37	Clifford, the Big Red Dog
36	Morris the Moose
35	The Cat in the Hat
34	Are You My Mother?
*Average text difficulty 33	Ranger Dan
32	
31	Green Eggs and Ham

An Anthology for Reading Apprenticeship: DRP Readability Ratings

Part I: Literacy and Identity

"Sharon Cho," from *Speaking of Reading*   54
   Sharon Cho

"Kevin Clarke," from *Speaking of Reading*   52
   Kevin Clarke

"Inside Out", from *The Circuit: Stories from the Life of a
   Migrant Child*   52
   Francisco Jiménez

From *The Acts of King Arthur and His
   Noble Knights*   60
   John Steinbeck

"My Back Pages," from *The Most Wonderful Books: Writers
   on Discovering the Pleasures of Reading*   60
   Greg Sarris

"Seis," from *Bless Me, Ultima*   46
   Rudolfo A. Anaya

"Discovering Books," from *Black Boy: A Record of
   Childhood and Youth*   51
   Richard Wright

"The Gift of Reading," from *Better Than Life*   49
  Daniel Pennac

"Coming into Language," from *Doing Time*:
  Twenty-Five Years of Prison Writing   62
  Jimmy Santiago Baca

"Silence," from *Woman Warrior*   54
  Maxine Hong Kingston

"Aria: A Memory of a Bilingual Childhood,"
  from *Hunger of Memory: The Education of*
  Richard Rodriguez: An Autobiography   59
  Richard Rodriguez

"Reading Has Always Been My Home," from *How Reading*
  Changed My Life   64
  Anna Quindlen

"Brownsville Schooldays," from *A Walker in*
  the City   64
  Alfred Kazin

Part II: Literacy and Power

"Gary Lee," from *Speaking of Reading*   50
  Gary Lee

"Two Ways to Be a Warrior," from *Luis Rodriguez: Writer,*
  Community Leader, Political Activist   56
  Michael Schwartz

"The Poets in the Kitchen," from *Reena and*
  Other Stories   62
  Paule Marshall

"Libraries and the Attack on Illiteracy"   67
  Timothy S. Healy

"Learning to Read," from *The Autobiography*
  of Malcolm X   60
    Malcolm X, Alex Haley

"In Conversation with Ernest J. Gaines"   59
    Adrianne Bee

"Learning to Read"   N.A.
    Frances E. W. Harper

"Precious Words"   N.A.
    Emily Dickinson

"Learning to Read and Write," from *Narrative of*
  The Life of Frederick Douglass   59
    Frederick Douglass

"India's Literacy Miracle"   62

"Interrogation," from *Son of the Revolution*   61
    Liang Heng, Judith Shapiro

"Reign of the Reader"   67
    M. Freeman

Part III: How We Read

"Gerald Eisman," from *Speaking of Reading*   60
    Gerald Eisman

"The Voice You Hear When You Read Silently"   N.A.
    Thomas Lux

"The Birth of an Alchemist," from *Better Than Life*   64
    Daniel Pennac

"Watch TV—In Your Head!"   58
    Jennifer Liu

"Tuning," from *The Winter Room*   57
    Gary Paulsen

"Superman and Me," from *The Most Wonderful
      Books: Writers on Discovering the Pleasures
      of Reading*   60
      Sherman Alexie

"How to Mark a Book"   58
      Mortimer Adler

"Learning to Read," from *A History of Reading*   68
      Alberto Manguel

"Three Wise Guys: *Un Cuento de Navidad/*
      A Christmas Story"   56
      Sandra Cisneros

"The New Case for Latin"   63
      Mike Eskenazi

"No Words," from *Wild Country: Outdoor Poems*
      for Young People   N.A.
      David Harrison

"Teaching People to Hate Literature"   65
      Matthew S.

"Team Xerox"   66
      Chris Taylor

"Private Reading," from *A History of Reading*   64
      Alberto Manguel

Part IV: Breaking Codes

"Susan Schulter," from *Speaking of Reading*   57
      Susan Schulter

"Important: Read This First"   63
      Frank Cammuso, Hart Seely

"The Secret Language of Custom"   56
      Evelyn H.

"Language Heads Down the Rabbit Hole"   67
    John Schwartz

"Cinematic Grammar," from *Reading the Movies:*
    Twelve Great Films on Video and How to Teach Them   63
    William V. Costanzo

"Hip-Hop Becoming a Worldwide Language
    for Youth Resistance"   70

"Double-Talk"   67
    Rick Bass

"Technicality," from *Science and Language Links: Classroom*
    Implications   69
    Johanna Scott

"Comic Books," from *A Book of Puzzlements:*
    Play and Invention with Language   59
    Herbert Kohl

Notes

Chapter One

1. See, for example, K. Haycock, "Closing the Achievement Gap," *Educational Leadership* (Mar. 2001): 6–11. G. A. Hull and M. Rose, "Rethinking Remediation: Toward a Social-Cognitive Understanding of Problematic Reading and Writing," *Written Communication* 8 (1989): 139–154.

2. J. Guthrie and A. Wigfield, "Engagement and Motivation in Reading," in M. L. Kamil, P. B. Mosenthal, P. D. Pearson, and R. Barr (eds.), *Handbook of Reading Research* (Mahwah, N.J.: Erlbaum, 2000), pp. 403–422.

3. P. L. Donahue, K. E. Voelkl, J. R. Campbell, and J. Mazzeo, *The NAEP 1998 Reading Report Card for the Nation and the States* (Washington, D.C.: National Center for Education Statistics, 1999).

4. See, for example, J. Davidson and D. Koppenhaver, *Adolescent Literacy: What Works and Why*, 2nd ed. (New York: Garland Publishing, 1993). E. B. Moje, J. P. Young, J. E. Readence, and D. W. Moore, "Reinventing Adolescent Literacy for New Times: Perennial and Millennial Issues," *Journal of Adolescent and Adult Literacy* 43 (2000): 400–410.

5. C. Greenleaf, R. Schoenbach, C. Cziko, and F. Mueller, "Apprenticing Adolescents to Academic Literacy," *Harvard Educational Review* 71 (2001): 79–129.

6. M. Clay, *Becoming Literate: The Construction of Inner Control* (Portsmouth, N.H.: Heinemann, 1991), p. 317.

Chapter Two

1. Studying Literature in a Heterogeneous Classroom," in S. W. Freedman, E. Simons, J. Kalnin, A. Casareno, and the M-Class Teams, *Inside City Schools: Investigating Literacy in Multicultural Classrooms* (New York: Teachers College Press, 1999).

Chapter Three

1. R. Schoenbach, C. Greenleaf, C. Cziko, and L. Hurwitz, *Reading for Understanding: A Guide to Improving Reading in Middle and High School Classrooms* (San Francisco: Jossey-Bass, 1999).

2. T. Rafael, "Question-Answering Strategies for Children," The Reading Teacher, 1982, 36, 186–190.

3. H. Daniels, *Literature Circles: Voice and Choice in the Student-Centered Classroom* (York, M.E.: Stenhouse Publications, 1994).

Chapter Six

1. See, for example, P. D. Pearson and L. G. Fielding, "Reading Comprehension: What Works," *Educational Leadership* (Feb. 1994): 62–68. J. F. Baumann and A. M. Duffy, *Engaged Reading for Pleasure and Learning: A Report from the National Reading Research Center* (Athens, Ga.: National Reading Research Center, 1997).

2. J. T. Guthrie and A. Wigfield (eds.), *Reading Engagement: Motivating Readers Through Integrated Instruction* (Newark, Del.: International Reading Association, 1997).

3. J. Edmondson and P. Shannon, "The Will of the People," in R. Allington, *Big Brother and the National Reading Curriculum: How Ideology Trumped Evidence* (Portsmouth, N.H.: Heinemann, 2002), pp. 224–231.

4. C. Lee, "A Culturally Based Cognitive Apprenticeship: Teaching African American High School Students Skills in Literary Interpretation," *Reading Research Quarterly* 30 (1995): 608–630.

5. J. Guthrie and A. Wigfield (see chap 1, n. 2)

Appendix D

1. K. Kinsella, "Initiating ESL Students to the Cooperative College Classroom," Cooperative Learning and College Teaching, 5(3), 6–10, in *Reading for Understanding*, p. 102.

Appendix E

1. N. Atwell, *In the Middle: New Understandings About Writing, Reading, and Learning*, 2nd ed. (Portsmouth, N.H.: Heinemann, 1998).

Bibliography

Professional Reading

Allen, J. *Leading Adolescents to Lifelong Literacy*. Portsmouth, N.H.: Heinemann, 1995.

Atwell, N. *In the Middle: New Understandings About Writing and Learning*. (2nd ed.) Portsmouth, N.H.: Heinemann, 1998.

Bascove (ed.). *Where Books Fall Open: A Reader's Anthology of Wit and Passion*. Lincoln, Mass.: Godine, 2001.

Beck, I. L., and others. *Questioning the Author: An Approach for Enhancing Student Engagement with Text*. Newark, Del.: International Reading Association, 1997.

Beers, K. *When Kids Can't Read—What Teachers Can Do: A Guide for Teachers 6–12*. Portsmouth, N.H.: Heinemann,

Billmeyer, R., and Barton, M. L. *Teaching Reading in the Content Areas: If Not Me, Then Who?* Aurora, Colo.: MCREL–Mid-continent Regional Educational Laboratory, 1998.

Burke, J. *I Hear America Reading: Why We Read—What We Read*. Portsmouth, N.H.: Heinemann, 1999.

Burke, J. *The English Teacher's Companion: A Complete Guide to Classroom Curriculum and the Profession*. Portsmouth, N.H.: Heinemann, 1999.

Burke, J. *Reader's Handbook: A Student Guide for Reading and Learning, Grades 9–12*. Boston: Houghton Mifflin, 2002.

Burke, J. *Illuminating Texts: How to Teach Students to Read the World*. Portsmouth, N.H.: Heinemann, 2001.

California Department of Education. *Strategic Teaching and Learning, Standards-Based Instruction to Promote Content Literacy in Grades Four Through Twelve*. Sacramento: State of California, 2000.

Chevigny, B. G. (ed.). *Doing Time: Twenty-Five Years of Prison Writing*. New York: Arcade, 1999.

Costanzo, W. *Reading the Movies: Twelve Great Films on Video and How to Teach Them*. Urbana, Ill.: National Council of Teachers of English, 1992.

Daniels, H. *Literature Circles: Voice and a Choice in Book Clubs and Reading Groups*. (2nd ed.) Portland, Me.: Stenhouse, 2002.

Dorris, M., and Buchwald, E. (eds.). *The Most Wonderful Books: Writers on Discovering the Pleasures of Reading*. Minneapolis, Minn.: Milkweed Editions, 1997.

Fadiman, A. *Ex Libris: Confessions of a Common Reader*. New York: Farrar, Straus & Giroux, 1998.

Fielding, A., and Schoenbach, R. (eds.). *Building Academic Literacy: An Anthology for Reading Apprenticeship*. San Francisco: Jossey-Bass, 2003.

Finn, P. *Literacy with an Attitude: Educating Working-Class Children in Their Own Self-Interest*. Albany: State University of New York Press, 1999.

Gilbar, S. (ed.). *The Open Door: When Writers First Learned to Read*. Lincoln, Mass.: Godine, 1989.

Gilbar, S. (ed.). *Reading in Bed: Personal Essays on the Glories of Reading*. Lincoln, Mass.: Godine, 1995.

Harper, M. S., and Walton, A. (eds.). *Every Shut Eye Ain't Asleep: An Anthology of Poetry by African Americans Since 1945*. New York: Little, Brown, 1994.

Harvey, S., and Goudivis, A. *Strategies That Work: Teaching Comprehension to Enhance Understanding*. Portland, Me.: Stenhouse, 2000.

Keene, E. O., and Zimmerman, S. *Mosaic of Thought: Teaching Comprehension in a Reader's Workshop*. Portsmouth, N.H.: Heinemann, 1997.

Kohl, H. *A Book of Puzzlements: Play and Invention with Language*. New York: Schocken Books, 1981.

Lamb, B. *Booknotes: America's Finest Authors on Reading, Writing, and the Power of Ideas*. New York: Random House, 1997.

Literacy and Learning in Secondary Schools. Newark, Del.: International Reading Association, 2000.

Manguel, A. *A History of Reading*. New York: Viking Press, 1996.

Mazer, A. (ed.). *Going Where I'm Coming From: Memoirs of American Youth: A Multicultural Anthology*. New York: Persea Books, 1995.

McCloud, S. *Understanding Comics: The Invisible Art*. New York: HarperCollins, 1993.

Moje, E.B.M. *"All the Stories That We Have": Adolescents' Insights About Literacy*

and Learning in Secondary Schools. Newark, Del.: International Reading
Association, 2000.

Pennac, D. *Better Than Life*. Ottawa: Coach House Press, 1994.

Power, B. M., Wilhelm, J. D., and Chandler, K. (eds.). *Reading Stephen King:
Issues of Censorship, Student Choice, and Popular Literature*. Urbana, Ill.:
National Council of Teachers of English, 1997.

Quindlen, A. *How Reading Changed My Life*. New York: Ballantine, 1998.

Rabinowitz, P. *Before Reading: Narrative Conventions and the Politics of Interpretation*. Ithaca, N.Y.: Cornell University Press, 1987.

Robb, L., Klemp, R., and Schwartz, W. *The Reader's Handbook: A Student
Guide for Reading and Learning, Grades 6–8*. Boston: Houghton Mifflin,
2002.

Rose, M. *Lives on the Boundary: A Moving Account of the Struggles and Achieve-
ments of America's Educational Underclass*. New York: Penguin Books,
1980.

Rosenthal, N. *Speaking of Reading*. Portsmouth, N.H.: Heinemann, 1995.

Schoenbach, R., Greenleaf, C., Cziko, C., and Hurwitz, L. *Reading for Understanding: A Guide to Improving Reading in Middle and High School Classrooms*. San Francisco: Jossey-Bass, 1999.

Scholes, R. *Protocols of Reading*. New Haven, Conn.: Yale University Press, 1989.

Schwartz, L. S. *Ruined by Reading: A Life in Books*. Boston: Beacon Press, 1996.

Scott, J. (ed.). *Science and Language Links: Classroom Implications*. Portsmouth,
N.H.: Heinemann, 1993.

Shwartz, R. B. *For the Love of Books: 115 Celebrated Writers on the Books They
Love Most*. New York: Grosset & Dunlap, 1999.

Smith, M. W., Wilhelm, J. D., and Newkirk, T. *Reading Don't Fix No Chevys:
Literacy in the Lives of Young Men*. Portsmouth, N.H.: Heinemann, 2002.

Taylor, D. (ed.). *Many Families, Many Literacies: An International Declaration of
Principles*. Portsmouth, N.H.: Heinemann, 1997.

Thompson, E. (ed.). *The Mercury Reader, 2000 Edition*. Boston: Pearson Custom
Publishing, 2001.

Tovani, C. *I Read It, But I Don't Get It: Comprehension Strategies for Adolescent
Readers*. Portland, Me.: Stenhouse, 2000.

Wilhelm, J. D. *"You Gotta Be the Book": Teaching Engaged and Reflective Reading
with Adolescents*. New York: Teachers College Press, 1997.

Wilhelm, J. D., Baker, T. N., and Dube, J. *Strategic Reading: Guiding Students to
Lifelong Literacy 6–12*. Portsmouth, N.H.: Boynton/Cook, 2001.

Woolf, V. *The Common Reader*. Orlando, Fla.: Harcourt Brace, 1948.

Web Resources

Educators for Social Responsibility, esrnational.org/. ESR's mission is to make teaching social responsibility a core practice in education so that young people develop the convictions and skills needed to shape a safe, sustainable, democratic, and just world.

MarcoPolo: Internet Content for the Classroom, marcopolo-education.org/. Provides standards-based Internet content and professional development to K–12 teachers and students throughout the United States.

McREL, Mid-continent Research for Education and Learning, mcrel.org/. Offers quality resources on literacy across curriculums.

North Central Regional Educational Laboratory, ncrel.org/. Presents resources and programs that can be used to improve the reading achievement of all students.

ReadWriteThink, readwritethink.org/. A partnership of the International Reading Association, the National Council of Teachers of English, and the MarcoPolo Education Foundation. Its mission is to provide educators and students with access to the highest-quality practices and resources in reading and language arts instruction through free Internet-based content.

SERVE: Improving Learning through Research and Development, serve.org/. Offers a literacy project.

Reading for Students

Allen, W. *Without Feathers*. New York: Random House, 1972.

Anaya, R. *Bless Me Ultima*. New York: Warner Books, 1994.

Bradby, M. *More Than Anything Else*. London: Orchard Books, 1995.

Brown, C. *Manchild in the Promised Land*. New York: Penguin Books, 1965.

Calvino, I. *If on a Winter's Night a Traveler*. Orlando, Fla.: Harcourt Brace, 1981.

Cofer, J. O. *Silent Dancing: A Partial Remembrance of a Puerto Rican Childhood*. Houston: Arte Publico Press, 1990.

Douglass, F. *The Life and Times of Frederick Douglass*. New York: Pathway Press, 1941.

Grimes, N. *Jazmin's Notebook*. New York: Puffin Books, 1998.

Heng, L., and Shapiro, J. *Sons of the Revolution*. New York: Knopf, 1983.

Hinton, S. E. *The Outsiders*. New York: Puffin Books, 1997.

Hirsch, J. S. *Hurricane: The Miraculous Journey of Ruben Carter*. Boston: Houghton Mifflin, 2000.

Ho, M. *The Clay Marble*. New York: Farrar, Straus & Giroux, 1991.

Holliday, L. (ed.). *Dreaming in Color, Living in Black and White: Our Own Stories of Growing Up Black in America*. New York: Pocket Books, 2000.

Hong Kingston, M. *Woman Warrior*. New York: Knopf, 1990.

Jimenez, F. *Breaking Through: Sequel to* The Circuit. Boston: Houghton Mifflin, 2001.

Jimenez, F. *The Circuit: Stories from the Life of a Migrant Child*. Albuquerque: University of New Mexico Press, 1997.

Jordan, J. *Soldier: A Poet's Childhood*. Basic Civitas Books, 2000.

Jordan, V. E., Jr., with Gordon-Reed, A. *Vernon Can Read: A Memoir*. Washington, D.C.: Public Affairs Press, 2000.

Kazin, A. *A Walker in the City*. New York: Grove Atlantic, 1951.

Lee, H. (ed.). *The Secret Self 1: Short Stories by Women*. London: Everyman, 1985.

Malcolm X, with Haley, A. *The Autobiography of Malcolm X*. New York: Ballantine Books, 1964.

Mazer, A. (ed.). *Going Where I'm Coming From: Memoirs of American Youth: A Multicultural Anthology*. New York: Persea Books, 1995.

McCurdy, M. (ed.). *Escape from Slavery: The Boyhood of Frederick Douglass in His Own Words*. New York: Knopf, 1994.

Ohanian, S. *Ask Ms. Class*. Portland, Me.: Stenhouse, 1995.

Paulsen, G. *The Winter Room*. New York: Bantam Books, 1989.

Paulsen, G. *Nightjohn*. New York: Bantam Books, 1993.

Pelzer, D. *A Child Called "It": One Child's Courage to Survive*. Deerfield Beach, Fla.: Health Communications, 1995.

Poitier, S. *The Measure of a Man: A Spiritual Autobiography*. New York: Harper-Collins, 2001.

Polacco, P. *Thank You Mr. Falker*. New York: Philomel Books, 1998.

Rodriguez, L. J. *Always Running: La Vida Loca, Gang Days in L.A.* New York: Touchstone, 1994.

Rodriguez, L. J. *It Doesn't Have to Be This Way: A Barrio Story*. Berkeley, Calif.: Children's Book Press, 1999.

Rodriguez, R. *Hunger of Memory: The Education of Richard Rodriguez: An Autobiography*. New York: Bantam Books, 1982.

Saldana, Jr., R. *The Jumping Tree: A Novel*. New York: Delacorte Press, 2001.

Salisbury, G. *Blue Skin of the Seas*. New York: Dell, 1992.

Schwartz, M. *Luis Rodriguez: Writer, Community Leader, Political Activist*. Austin, Tex.: Steck-Vaughn, 1997.

Sendak, M. *Where the Wild Things Are*. New York: HarperCollins, 1963.

Shelley, M. *Frankenstein*. New York: St. Martin's Press, 1992.

Spinelli, J. *Maniac Magee*. New York: Little, Brown, 1990.

Wright, R. *Black Boy: A Record of Childhood and Youth*. HarperCollins, 1937.

About the Editors

Audrey Fielding is a consultant with the Strategic Literacy Initiative of WestEd and the Bay Area Writing Program. She has been involved in English language arts instruction as a teacher, resource teacher, and bilingual teacher at the middle and high school levels in Costa Rica and the San Francisco Bay Area for a number of years. For the past ten years, she has worked as a literacy coach with teachers in Northern California, El Salvador, and Namibia. Her writing has appeared in National and Bay Area Writing Project publications, the National and Northern California Peace Corps Newsletters, and *Sistersong: Women Across Cultures*, a literary journal. She has a master's degree in secondary education from San Francisco State University and is a graduate of the Master of Arts in Writing Program at the University of San Francisco.

Ruth Schoenbach is codirector of the Strategic Learning Initiative at WestEd. She has coauthored *Reading for Understanding: A Guide to Improving Reading in Middle and High School Classrooms* (Jossey-Bass, 1999) and a number of articles, including "Apprenticing Adolescent Readers to Academic Texts" (*Harvard Educational Review*, Spring 2001). From 1988 to 1996, she directed the Humanities Education, Research, and Language Development Project in the San

Francisco Unified School District, where she had worked previously as a classroom teacher and curriculum developer. She has a master's degree from the Harvard Graduate School of Education in teaching, curriculum, and learning environments.

Marean Jordan is the director of professional development for the Strategic Literacy Initiative at WestEd. Previously, she served as co-director of the Alliance for Collaborative Change in School Systems (ACCESS) at the Lawrence Hall of Science, a University of California, Berkeley partnership initiative with Oakland and San Francisco school districts supporting secondary instructional and curriculum improvement in mathematics, English-language arts, and social studies. She has many years of experience teaching English and writing, developing curriculum, and planning and facilitating professional development for educators in K–12 and higher education. She has a B.A. and M.A. in English from San Francisco State University.

About the Sponsor

WestEd is a nonprofit education research, development, and service agency headquartered in San Francisco, with offices in California and throughout the U.S. WestEd's researchers and policy analysts conduct wide-ranging programs aimed at improving education and other opportunities for children, youths, and adults.

The Strategic Literacy Initiative (SLI) is a collaborative research, development, and service organization based in the Oakland, California WestEd office. It works with educators and communities to develop the literacy skills of adolescents; its mission is to expand the academic, creative, career, and civic opportunities of young people through higher-level literacy development.

The SLI develops text and videotaped literacy case studies of adolescent readers, provides inquiry-based professional development for teams of middle and high school teachers, provides teachers with access to relevant research and resources, and studies the impact of its programs on student and teacher learning.

The initiative is supported through funding from the Stuart Foundation, the William and Flora Hewlett Foundation, the Carnegie Corporation, the Walter S. Johnson Foundation, the Stupski Family Foundation, and the W. Clement and Jessie V. Stone Foundation, in addition to contracts with schools, districts, and county offices of education.

Index

A

Abbott Middle School (San Mateo, California), 91, 101, 102

Academic literacy: definition of, 4; four-unit overview matrix, 126–129; impact of, on student reading, 7; and Reading History (Unit Three), 128; and Reading Media (Unit Two), 127; and Reading Science and Technology (Unit Four), 129; and Reading Self and Society (Unit One), 126; student competencies, 149–150; three goals of, 5

Academic Literacy course: challenges and next steps for, at Jefferson High School, 89–90; and classroom interactions, 118–121; creating, at Jefferson High School, 48–53; curriculum design guidelines for, 111–123; in English, 133–135; first four weeks of Moulthrop's, 22–23; introduction to, 1–9; and literacy identity, 53–79; new directions for, 122–123; and school wide design, 121–122; timeline, 132; year one of, 48–50; year three of, 52–53; year two of, 50–52

Achievement gap, 1

Acts of King Arthur and His Noble Knights (Steinbeck), 103, 155

Adler, M., 158

Advanced Placement (AP), 47, 48

African American students, 1, 5, 115

Alexie, S., 158

Always Running: La Vida Loca (Rodriguez), 17, 21, 23, 43, 103

American Academy for Advancement of Science, 118

Anaya, R. A., 155

Anthem (Rand), 59

"Aria: A Memory of a Bilingual Childhood" (Rodriguez), 54, 156

Atwell, N., 7, 81

Autobiography of Malcolm X (Malcolm X and Haley), 21, 23, 157

B

Baca, J. S., 54, 103, 156

Baker, E., 13–15, 47, 112

Bass, R., 159

Bee, A., 157

Better Than Life (Pennac), 156, 157

Bimbi, 33

Black Boy: A Record of Childhood and Youth (Wright), 155

Bless Me, Ultima (Anaya), 155

Brown, C., 21

Building Academic Literacy: A Reading Apprenticeship Anthology (Fielding and Schoenback), 17, 20, 21, 25, 31, 60, 68, 111, 112, 153

C

California Achievement Test (CAT), 54, 55, 73, 74
Cammuso, F., 158
Charlotte's Web (White), 8
Child Called "It": One Child's Courage To Survive, A (Pelzer), 89
Chinese American students, 5
Cho, S., 21, 155
"Cinematic Grammar" (Costanzo), 159
Circuit: Stories from the Life of a Migrant Child (Jiménez), 155
Cisneros, S., 134, 158
Clarke, K., 21, 155
Clay Marble (Ho), 108
"Comic Books" (Kohl), 159
"Coming into Language" (Baca), 54, 103, 104, 156
Comprehension strategies, 14–15
Conferences, 79–87; formal, 83–85; informal, 81–83; think-aloud, 85–87. *See also* Instruction, individualizing
Convicted in the Womb (Upchurch), 54
Costanzo, W. V., 159
Cultural modeling, 115
Curriculum overview (Unit One), 52–53, 54–57
Cziko, C., 4, 5, 9, 17, 37, 48, 90, 108, 111, 121, 122, 129

D

Degrees of Reading Power (DRP) test, 7, 8, 54, 55, 74, 78, 151–153; scale of readability, 154
Dickinson, E., 157
Doing Time: Twenty-Five Years of Prison Writing (Baca), 156
"Double-Talk" (Bass), 159
Douglass, F., 21, 37, 45, 157
Dr. Seuss, 61

E

Eisman, G., 157
Escape from Slavery (Douglass), 21, 23, 37–40, 157

Eskenazi, M., 158
Expectations, 63–73, 63–73

F

Filipino students, 5
Fitzhugh, L., 59–60
Frankenstein (Shelley), 89
Freeman, M., 157

G

"Gary Lee" (Lee), 21, 23, 24–31, 103, 156
"Gerald Eisman" (Eisman), 157
Give one, get one technique, 37
Goals: poster displaying sample, 80–81; San Lorenzo High School, 20–21
Graphic organizers, 140–141
Greenleaf, C., 4, 7, 9, 17, 37, 48, 90, 108, 111, 121, 122, 129
Groups, reading in, 39–41

H

Haley, A., 21, 157
Harper, F., 21, 157
Harriet the Spy (Fitzhugh), 59–60
Harrison, D., 158
Healy, T. S., 156
Heng, L., 157
Hinton, S. E., 61
Historical knowledge, 138
History detectives, 90, 92
Ho, M., 108
Homework, reading for, 42
House on Mango Street (Cisneros), 134
How Reading Changed My Life (Quindlen), 156
"How To Mark a Book" (Adler), 158
Hunger of Memory: An Autobiography (Rodriguez), 156
Hurwitz, L., 4, 9, 17, 37, 48, 90, 108, 111, 121, 122, 129

I

I Wanna Be Average (Rose), 54
"Important: Read This First" (Cammuso and Seely), 158

"In Conversation with Ernest J. Gaines" (Bee), 157
In the Middle: New Understandings About Writing and Learning (Atwell), 81
Instruction, individualizing, 79–89; and conferencing, 79–87; and formal conferences, 83–85; and informal conferencing with students, 81–83; and literature circles, 88–89; and reading letters, 87–88; and reviews of progress, 87; and think-aloud conferences, 85–87; and think-aloud evaluation form, 86

J

Jefferson High School (Daly City, California), 47; creating Academic Literacy course for, 48–53
Jiminéz, F., 155
Jordan, J., 21
Journals, 28–30

K

Kazin, A., 156
"Kevin Clarke" (Clarke), 21, 23, 155
Kingston, M. H., 21, 156
Kohl, H., 159

L

"Language Heads Down the Rabbit Hole" (Schwartz), 159
Latino adolescents, 1, 5
Learning goals, 77–79
"Learning to Read and Write" (Douglass), 21, 157
"Learning to Read" (Harper), 21, 38, 157
"Learning to Read" (Malcolm X and Haley), 21, 31–35, 37, 40, 54, 60, 61, 64, 65, 157
"Learning to Read" (Manguel), 158
Lee, C., 115
Lee, G., 21, 156
Lee, H., 59
Lessons from Reading Apprenticeship Classrooms, 4

Levine, M., 139
"Libraries and the Attack on Illiteracy" (Healy), 156
Library visits, 63
Literary performance, scaffolding, 15
Literature circles, 88–89
Liu, J., 157
Logs, metacognitive, 68–72, 107–108, 115
Louis Rodriguez: Writer, Community Leader, Political Activist (Schwartz), 156
Lux, T., 54, 91, 102, 104, 157

M

Malcolm X, 21, 45, 54, 60, 61, 64, 65, 157
Manchild in the Promised Land (Brown), 21, 23
Manguel, A., 158
Marshall, P., 156
Matthew S., 158
Mead, M., 47
Messina, L., 13–15, 47, 112
Metacognition: developing, 24–36; heart of, 71; note taking and journal response in, 28–30; resource maps and think-aloud process in, 31–34; and useful notation, 30–31
Metacognitive conversations, 10, 12–14
Metacognitive logs, 68–72, 107–108, 115
Mini-lessons, 65–67
Most Wonderful Books: Writers on Discovering the Pleasures of Reading (Sarris), 155
Mother Goose, 62
Moulthrop, D., 13, 14, 17, 22, 133

N

National Association of Science Teachers, 118
National Educational Assessment Program (NEAP), 2
National Institute on Reading Apprenticeship, 4, 91

"New Case for Latin, The" (Eskenazi), 158
"No Words" (Harrison), 158
Notation, 28–31

O

Old Yeller (Gipson), 8
Orta, C., 13, 14, 91, 101
Outsiders, The (Hinton), 61

P

Paulsen, G., 157
Pelzer, D., 89
Pennac, D., 156, 157
Personal reading history maps, 62–63
Play-Doh, 36
"Precious Words" (Dickinson), 157
Prince, The (Machiavelli), 8
"Private Reading" (Manguel), 158
Problem-solving strategies, 36–42

Q

Questions, 37–39; and question-answer relationship, 41–42
Quick writes, 64
Quindlen, A., 156

R

Rand, A., 59
Readers: and awakening reader within, 58–63; becoming, 43–45; developing confidence of, 41–46; and good reader strategies, 106; poster displaying sample goals for, 80–81
Reading: and choosing books, 61–62; impact of Academic Literacy on student, 7; letters, 87–88; and library visits, 63; and personal reading history maps, 62–63; and sharing favorite books, 61; sharing stories about, 59–61; student, survey, 143–147
Reading Apprenticeship: dimensions of, 11, 11–13; extending, 105–107;

framework, 111; introduction to, 9–13, 9–13
Reading Apprenticeship classrooms: and building vocabulary, 104; and capturing reading process, 104–105; creating, 101–110; and explicit teaching of comprehension strategies in context of meaningful texts, 14–15; and extending reading apprenticeship, 105–107; lessons from, 13–15; and making invisible visible, 102–104; and metacognitive conversation, 13–14; and smart routines, 15; and student agency, 14; teaching strategies for, 109–110; and using metacognitive logs, 107–108
Reading for Understanding: A Guide to Improving Reading in Middle and High School Classrooms (Schoenbach, Greenleaf, Cziko, and Hurwitz), 4, 9, 17, 37, 48, 90, 108, 111, 121, 122, 129
Reading History (Unit Three), 6, 128, 137–141
Reading letters, 87–88
Reading Media (Unit Two), 6, 127
Reading process: and assessing understanding, 97–99; beginning exploration of, 93–95; capturing, 104–105; and making meaning from texts, 91–93; and performing poem, 95–97
Reading Science and Technology (Unit Four), 6, 129
Reading Self and Society, 6; and creating sense of safety, 21, 24; final assessment for, 43–45; goals for, 20–21; introducing, 20–24; overview matrix, 126
Reciprocal Teaching (RT), 7, 14, 134, 135, 139
Reena and Other Stories (Marshall), 156
"Reign of the Reader" (Freeman), 157
Research skills, 139

Resource maps, 31–34, 62–63; example of, 34, 35
Rodriguez, L., 17, 21, 45, 103, 156
Rodriguez, R., 54, 156
Romeo and Juliet (Shakespeare), 20
Rose, M., 54
Routines, 63–73
"Row, Row, Row Your Boat," 95–96

S

Safety, sense of, 21, 24
San Francisco Bay Area, 4, 48
San Lorenzo High School (San Lorenzo, California), 17, 19–20, 133
Santayana, G., 137
Sarris, G., 155
SAT 9, 74
Scaffolding, 15, 115
Scarlet Letter, The (Hawthorne), 8
Schoenbach, R., 1, 4, 9, 17, 37, 48, 90, 108, 111, 121, 122, 129
Schulter, S., 158
Schwartz, J., 159
Schwartz, M., 156
Scott, J., 159
"Secret Language of Custom, The" (Evelyn H.), 158
Seely, H., 158
Sendak, M., 61
Shapiro, J., 157
Share-outs, class, 72–73
"Sharon Cho" (Cho), 21, 23, 42, 155
Shelley, M., 89
"Silence" (Kingston), 21, 156
Smart routines, 15
Smith, A., 14, 91, 101
Soldier: A Poet's Childhood (Jordan), 21, 23, 35, 36
Son of the Revolution (Heng and Shapiro), 157
Speaking of Reading, 156, 157
Standardized reading comprehension tests, 8
Steinbeck, J., 103, 155
Strategic Literacy Initiative (SLI;

WestEd), 1, 2, 7, 9, 91, 101, 151
Students: assessing reading abilities and reading backgrounds of, 73–77; informal conferencing with, 81–83; responses to mini-lessons, 66–67; and student agency, 14
"Superman and Me" (Alexie), 158
Surveys, student responses to reading, 8–9
"Susan Schulter," 158
Sustained silent reading (SSR), 6, 57, 68–70, 72, 81, 82, 114, 115, 134, 139
Swing Kids (documentary film), 117

T

Taylor, C., 158
"Teaching People to Hate Literature" (Matthew S.), 158
Teaching strategies, 109–110; and common pitfalls, 120
"Team Xerox" (Taylor), 158
"Technicality" (Scott), 159
Tests, standardized, 8
Texts: comprehension strategies in context of meaningful, 14–15; engaging students in working with, 17–46; laying groundwork for talking to, 26–27; making sense of, 66
Think-aloud process, 31; evaluation form, 86; introducing, 34–36; and think-aloud conferences, 85–87
"Three Wise Guys: *Un Cuento de Navidad*/A Christmas Story" (Cisneros), 158
Thurgood Marshall Academic High School (San Francisco), 5, 7, 116, 117
To Kill a Mockingbird (Lee), 8, 59
Touchstone Applied Science Association (TASA), 151–153

U

Understanding, assessing, 97–99
Upchurch, C., 54
Useful notation, 30–31

V

Vocabulary, building, 104
"Voice You Hear When You Read
    Silently, The" (Lux), 54, 91–93, 96,
    97, 102–104, 104, 157

W

Walker in the City (Kazin), 156
Warm-ups, 64–65
"Watch TV-In Your Head" (Liu), 157

Wave, The (documentary film),
    117
WestEd, 1, 11
Where the Wild Things Are (Sendak),
    61
Winter Room, The (Paulsen), 157
Woman Warrior (Kingston), 21, 23,
    156
Word knowledge, 138
Wright, R., 155

Reading for Understanding: A Guide to Improving Reading in Middle and High School Classrooms

Ruth Schoenbach, Cynthia Greenleaf,
Christine Cziko, Lori Hurwitz
Copublished with WestEd
Paperback, December 1999, 240 pp., 8½ × 11,
$21.00, ISBN 0-7879-5045-9

This book introduces the nationally recognized Reading Apprenticeship™ instructional framework, a research-based model with a proven record of success in increasing the engagement and achievement of adolescent readers, including many considered "struggling" or disengaged students. Filled with vivid classroom lessons and exercises, the book shows teachers how to "apprentice" students to reading in the disciplines, an approach that demystifies the reading process for students so they can acquire the necessary motivational, cognitive, and knowledge-building strategies for comprehending diverse and challenging types of texts. The book also presents a detailed description of the pilot Academic Literacy curriculum, a year-long course in which a group of urban ninth-grade students made an average of two years' gain in reading comprehension. In addition, it shows how Reading Apprenticeship strategies can be embedded in science, math, English, and social studies classrooms, thus serving as a useful guide for teachers working across the curricula in grades 6–12.

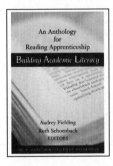

Building Academic Literacy: An Anthology for Reading Apprenticeship

Audrey Fielding and Ruth Schoenbach,
Editors
Copublished with WestEd
Paperback, April 2003, 304 pp., 6 × 9, $16.00
ISBN: 0-7879-6555-3

Featuring lively and provocative essays by such writers as Maxine Hong Kingston, Richard Wright, Sherman Alexie, and Richard Rodriguez, and covering a wide range of cultural and historical contexts, this thematically organized anthology invites middle and high school students to explore the questions of why and how we read, the connections between literacy, self-empowerment, academic success, and life achievement, and the different "codes" of meaning found across text genres and disciplines. Created as a resource for teachers interested in implementing the Academic Literacy curriculum as described in *Reading for Understanding*, the anthology can also serve as a valuable supplementary text in any classroom where teachers are looking for ways to engage adolescents in becoming motivated and strategic readers.

[Prices subject to change]